NO AR

COPING WHEN

You or

A Friend Is

HIV-Positive

Pat Kelly

THE ROSEN PUBLISHING GROUP, INC./NEW YORK

*Special thanks to Brenda Garza at the
Centers for Disease Control and Prevention (CDC)
for ensuring the accuracy of the technical sections of
this book.*

Published in 1995, 1998 by The Rosen Publishing Group, Inc.
29 East 21st Street, New York, NY 10010

Revised Edition 1998

Cover photo by Kim Sonsky

Library of Congress Cataloging-in-Publication Data
Kelly, Pat.
    Coping when you or a friend is HIV-positive / Pat Kelly.
        p.   cm.
    Includes bibliographical references and index.
    ISBN 0-8239-2626-5
    1. AIDS (Disease)—Juvenile literature.   2. HIV infections—
Juvenile literature.   I. Title.
RC607.A26K455 1995
362. 1'969792—dc20
                                                                95-8556
                                                                    CIP

ABOUT THE AUTHOR ◇

Pat Kelly works for Buistmore, Smythe, and McGee as a Software Specialist in Charleston, South Carolina. Ms. Kelly also volunteers in assisting low-income adults to improve their basic reading, writing, and math skills.

She graduated summa cum laude from the College of Charleston in 1989 with a BA in History and Political Science. She also has a joint master's degree from the University of Charleston and the University of South Carolina.

Over the years, Ms. Kelly has published writings ranging from fiction to editorials. She lives in Charleston with her husband, George, her two children, Demian and Adam, and a variety of pets.

Contents

Introduction

There is good and bad news about AIDS (acquired immune deficiency syndrome).

The good news is the discovery of powerful drugs for treating AIDS. The new drugs cannot prevent or cure the disease, but they can stop the growth of the disease in the infected person's body. With AIDS, this is real progress. For the first time since the epidemic began, AIDS patients are looking to the future with hope.

The bad news is that young people are still contracting AIDS at an alarming rate. In 1993, the number of reported AIDS cases among people aged thirteen to nineteen years old rose more than 200 percent. Recent years have shown no significant drop from the 1993 level. Four percent of all AIDS patients in the United States are under nineteen years old. Unfortunately, scientists are afraid that the real figure is significantly higher. This figure reflects only those teenagers who are aware that they have AIDS. Many more teenagers are likely to be infected with HIV, and don't know it yet. They will develop AIDS as they become older. The Centers for Disease Control and Prevention (CDC) estimate that teenagers now account for 20 percent of the total number of people in the United States with HIV.

Although some teens have started taking precautions against HIV, most have not. They seem to think "it will never happen" to them. They experiment with both sex and drugs, the two most common ways to contract HIV. Studies have shown that the average age at which a teenage boy has sex for the first time is fifteen; for teenage girls it is sixteen. In the United States, a teenage girl becomes pregnant every thirty seconds. Also, every year about 3 million teenagers contract sexually transmitted diseases (STDs) like gonorrhea and syphilis. HIV can also be sexually transmitted; in fact, it is most commonly spread through unprotected sexual contact.

HIV is also transmitted through the sharing of needles and syringes. Surveys have shown that 60 percent of all American high school seniors have experimented with illegal drugs, some by injection. Having unprotected sex with someone who uses intravenous (IV) drugs increases the chances of contracting HIV. Many teenage girls have contracted HIV from sexual partners who are intravenous drug users. In 1996, one quarter of all U.S. women with HIV were under eighteen.

There are several differences between being an adult with AIDS and a teenager with AIDS.

- More teenage cases are caused by hetero-sexual transmission than homosexual transmission.
- Teenagers generally do not show symptoms of the disease until they are adults.
- Teenagers with AIDS don't have the peer and community support that the adult community provides.
- Teenagers are rarely financially able to seek medical and psychological counseling, especially if they do not tell their parents about their HIV status.

A person who has HIV in the blood is said to be HIV-positive or seropositive; a person who does not have the virus is said to be HIV-negative or seronegative. Although some people who are HIV-positive never develop AIDS, many do, even if it is after a long period of time. If you are HIV-positive, it is something that you have to live with every day. HIV affects not only the infected person, but also the people who know and care about him or her. HIV is something young people would like to believe will never happen to them, but too often this is not the case.

Maya's Story

Maya was scared to go to the hospital. She had no idea what to say to her sister, Yvonne, and her new nephew. At twenty, Yvonne was five years older than Maya, and had just given birth to a baby boy.

A few days after she gave birth, Yvonne was told that her baby was HIV-positive, like Yvonne herself. Everyone in the family was shaken by the news. Yvonne had contracted the infection from Rick, her ex-husband, a drug user. Yvonne was scheduled to return home with her baby at the end of the week and Maya was afraid. She didn't know much about AIDS, but the stories she had heard frightened her.

The hospital visit went well until it was time to leave. Yvonne held out her arms for a hug, and Maya refused. She couldn't bring herself to hug Yvonne or even to say that she was glad Yvonne would be home soon.

On the way home, Maya started to cry. She loved her sister, but she was afraid to touch her. When her mother asked Maya what was wrong, she said, "Everything! The baby is HIV-positive; Yvonne is HIV-positive; and now I'm going to get sick and so are you." Maya's mother told her not to worry. "It is perfectly safe for you to hug your sister, and kiss your nephew," Maya's mother said. "In fact, I think it would really help them if you would. I think it would help you too." Maya tried to believe her, but that night she couldn't sleep. Her fears kept circling in her head. She was going to be living in a house of sick people; none of her friends would come over; and eventually she'd get sick just like Yvonne.

When Yvonne and the baby came home two days later, Maya refused to speak to Yvonne. She went to her room, slammed the door shut, and refused to come out.

You can see how much fear and confusion HIV can cause, even among people who love each other. The fact that Yvonne and her baby were HIV-positive was enough to make Maya afraid to be in the same room with them. She worsened her fears by withdrawing from her family. If she had asked more questions or tried to discuss her feelings, she might have felt more secure.

Unfortunately, like Maya, many people are afraid to discuss AIDS. They are afraid to talk about HIV. They base their knowledge upon news stories, old information, and incorrect myths. New advances in AIDS research are happening all the time. There are new, more effective treatments. The outlook is good. What was once inevitably fatal, is now, with the right treatment, often manageable. If you don't talk about it, you will never learn about these significant changes.

This book offers some basic information about HIV and AIDS. It offers some ways to help you cope when you or someone you know is HIV-positive. It discusses many of the legal, medical, social, and emotional issues that go along with being HIV-positive. And it provides up-to-date information about the latest developments in tests and treatments for HIV. Now, as never before, the more you know about HIV, the easier it is to cope with it.

CHAPTER 1

What Are HIV and AIDS?

HIV is *not* the same thing as AIDS. If you test positive for HIV, it does *not* mean you have AIDS. While many people who contract HIV go on to develop AIDS, many others have not. However, it is not possible to be diagnosed with AIDS without first being HIV-positive. Studies done of people with HIV in California in the late 1980s found that 36 percent of them developed AIDS within eight years, over 40 percent developed symptoms of other infections, and 20 percent continued to be symptom-free. The medical community is still searching for answers.

HIV stands for human immunodeficiency virus. It is a small, simple virus that is very difficult to control once it is in the body because it is a retrovirus. A retrovirus is able to use its own core to reproduce rather than having to use a host cell. HIV is made up mostly of proteins, some of which are P17, P18, P24, P25, gp41, and gp120. The virus infects the body when the gp120 pro-

teins attach themselves to body cells (host cells) containing the protein CD4. Not all cells have CD4, but some
cells in the brain, the lungs, the lower intestine, and the
bone marrow do. CD4 cells are also called white blood
cells or lymphocytes. Certain lymphocytes called T4
cells and T-helper cells are part of the body's immune
system. Once the virus has attached itself to a host cell, it
enters the host's nucleus (center of the cell) and changes
the genetic design of the cell. The infected cell may eventually break apart and release more HIV cells into the
body.

Because HIV attaches itself to the T4 cells or the T-
helper cells in the immune system, the body is unable to
fight back as it would against other viruses. Though new
drug treatments have led to dramatic improvements in the
health of many AIDS patients, the treatments cannot cure
the disease.

If you test positive for HIV, you are said to be HIV-
positive or seropositive. If you are asymptomatic, you have
no symptoms of HIV. But having no symptoms does not
mean that you do not have HIV. In fact, you probably
wouldn't even know you were seropositive if you hadn't
had a blood test. But even if you are asymptomatic, you
still can pass the virus to others. Actually, most of the
people who are HIV-positive now are asymptomatic. This
can be dangerous because they may not know they are
infected. They may unsuspectingly pass on the virus to
other people. That is why it is important to protect yourself against HIV no matter how you feel right now. You
can be asymptomatic for a long time. The average time
between diagnosis and the onset of symptoms is five to
eight years, but that time can be increased with proper
care. Also, the particular strain of HIV involved has some
bearing on how long a person can remain asymptomatic.

When you begin to show signs of HIV, you are said to be symptomatic. Some conditions that are associated with being HIV-symptomatic are fungus infections in the mouth, like thrush and oral hairy leukoplakia. Other conditions include chronic fever, chronic diarrhea, chronic fatigue, and weight loss. Before any of these conditions can be diagnosed as HIV-symptomatic, there must be no other reason for the symptoms than HIV. Oral hairy leukoplakia is found only in persons infected with HIV, but thrush, fatigue, weight loss, fever, and diarrhea may have other causes.

Many scientists believe that AIDS is the last stage of HIV infection, although that conclusion has recently been questioned. It is believed that certain cofactors may increase the possibility of HIV developing into AIDS. Three common cofactors include drugs, alcohol, and cigarettes. If you use any of these substances and are HIV-positive, you greatly increase your risk of developing AIDS. Stress and reinfection are other cofactors that may increase the danger of AIDS. Reinfection most commonly occurs when an HIV-positive person is exposed to HIV through having unprotected sex (sex without a condom) or sharing drug paraphernalia with someone who has HIV.

AIDS is a syndrome. That means that no specific symptom determines that you have AIDS. The Centers for Disease Control and Prevention (CDC) list a variety of diseases or opportunistic infections that can be included in a diagnosis of AIDS. See the Where to Go for Help section in this book for information on how to contact the CDC. Ask your health-care provider for further information about opportunistic infections and tumors. The list is always changing, with some infections being deleted and others being added.

Remember, people diagnosed with HIV and AIDS are living longer today than those of ten years ago. Every day, new information is gained about HIV and AIDS. The most important tool you can have is knowledge.

CHAPTER 2

Myths Surrounding HIV

Myth #1: You can catch AIDS by drinking out of the same glass as someone who is HIV-positive.

Reality: You do not "catch" AIDS. AIDS develops in people who are already HIV-positive. You cannot "catch" it by sharing utensils. You cannot "catch" AIDS by kissing or hugging someone who is HIV-positive. In fact, if you have a friend with HIV, touching and hugging your friend is a good way to show that you care and that you are aware of the myths surrounding HIV.

It is not easy to become infected with HIV. You cannot become infected with HIV by an insect bite or if someone who is HIV-positive spits at you. There are only three ways to contract HIV:

- through intrauterine transfer from mother to child before, during, or right after childbirth

- from the exchange of body fluids: blood and blood products, semen, vaginal secretions, or breast milk from someone who is already infected
- through the use of contaminated syringes or needles, which is another way to exchange body fluids.

As a teenager, you are at risk for contracting HIV if you have unprotected sex (sex without a condom) or share needles or syringes for drug use. Because you cannot tell if someone is HIV-positive just by looking at him or her, every time you engage in risky behavior you face the possibility of contracting HIV.

Myth #2: You can contract HIV when you donate blood or during a dental exam.

You are *not* at risk for contracting HIV when you donate blood. Medical personnel use a new disposable syringe for each donor. That means that the only body fluid in the syringe is your own. Before the American Red Cross began screening all donated blood for HIV antibodies, it was possible to contract the virus by receiving contaminated blood during a transfusion.

Many people with hemophilia, like Ryan White, contracted HIV from contaminated blood. Hemophilia is an inherited condition that prevents the blood from clotting. Only boys are born with hemophilia. People with hemophilia have to avoid any kind of injury, even small bruises. They often have to have blood transfusions to help their own blood clot more effectively. Ryan White contracted HIV during a blood transfusion to treat his hemophilia. Since 1985, all donated blood in the United States has been screened for HIV antibodies. There is still a possibility of infection from a transfusion if a donor has not yet developed the antibodies, but the screening process has reduced that possibility almost to zero.

No confirmed reports exist of infection by casual contact with someone who is HIV-positive. Kimberly Bergalis, a young woman from Florida, contracted HIV from her dentist. Several other people also learned they had contracted the virus after visiting the same dentist. When the news became public, there was great concern about what seemed to be the easy transmission of AIDS. Many people worried that it was possible to become infected just by having someone with AIDS perform simple services for them such as cleaning their teeth or serving them food.

A possible explanation for Ms. Bergalis's infection came from one of the dentist's former friends. He claimed that Dr. David Acer was very angry about having AIDS and became obsessed with making other people share his experience. According to his friend, he deliberately infected Ms. Bergalis and several other people by injecting his own infected blood cells into their gums. Dr. Acer died before this report came out, so there was no way to verify it. It has been challenged recently by some who claim that Ms. Bergalis and others lied about their earlier health risks. No matter which story is true, or even if neither one is true, it is highly unlikely that Dr. Acer's patients contracted AIDS just because he had AIDS. An exchange of body fluids had to occur.

The risk of contracting HIV at your dentist's office is very small. The law requires dentists to sterilize all equipment after each use. They are required to wear gloves and to wash their hands thoroughly before treating each patient. Dentists also throw away all one-use items like gloves, disposable syringes, and cotton swabs. Because contracting HIV requires an exchange of body fluids, the only way to be infected in the dentist's office is by accidentally coming in contact with contaminated blood. The precautions dentists take today mean that the only body fluids you are exposed to in the dental chair are your own.

Myth #3: You are safe from contracting HIV as long as you have sex only when you are having your period.

Reality: Because HIV is transmitted through vaginal secretions, semen, or blood, having sex when you are having your period is *not* a way to be safe. In fact, if you are an HIV-positive female, having unprotected sex when you are having your period is a good way to infect your partner.

HIV takes no time off. Avoiding HIV is not like avoiding pregnancy. Using diaphragms, spermicides, or birth control pills may diminish your chances of becoming pregnant, but they have absolutely no effect on HIV. Engaging in anal intercourse actually *increases* your chances of becoming infected. During anal sex, tissue is often torn, thus increasing the chances of mixing blood and semen. The only time you are really safe from becoming infected with HIV is when you don't have sex. If you do engage in sexual intercourse, you and your partner can improve both of your chances of being safe by *always* using a latex condom.

Myth #4: If you have sex with only one person, you are safe from getting HIV.

Reality: Having sex is one of the fundamental ways to contract HIV. If the one person you have sex with is infected, you may become infected as well. If the person you have sex with has had sex with someone who passed on the virus, or if that person is an intravenous drug user, your chances of contracting the virus increase.

By having sex with only one person (being monogamous), you may decrease your chances of becoming infected *only* if you know for sure that the person is free from the virus. If your partner engages in casual sex or intravenous drug use, your chances of getting the virus increase dramatically, even if you only have the one partner.

Remember, every time you have unprotected sex with a person, you are also having sex with everyone else who has had sex with that person. The only way to decrease your chances of becoming infected during sexual intercourse is to use a latex condom.

Myth #5: It is very dangerous to be around someone who is HIV-positive.

Reality: It is much more dangerous for the person who is HIV-positive to be around others. Because you cannot contract HIV through casual contact such as shaking hands or kissing, a person who is HIV-positive presents no danger to a person who is not infected unless they engage in unprotected sex or share needles or syringes. On the other hand, because people with HIV are more susceptible to diseases and opportunistic infections, they must be extra cautious when around someone who has even a cold or the flu. The immune system in an HIV-positive person is weak; he or she can easily contract a disease from someone else.

Remember, you cannot "catch" HIV, but you can "catch" a cold. A person who is HIV-positive faces danger from the people near him or her, not the other way around.

Myth #6: Someone who gets HIV is a bad person.

Reality: Diseases of any type have nothing to do with the kind of person you are. HIV is a virus. Viruses have no brains; they don't think. Viruses do not pick and choose who will offer them a home and who won't. All kinds of people are infected with HIV: grandmothers, newborn babies, religious people, hemophiliacs, teenagers, heterosexuals, homosexuals, men, women, boys, and girls. People of all colors and all backgrounds, good and bad, are susceptible to HIV.

Myth #7: Only homosexuals get HIV.

Reality: Anyone can get HIV, not just homosexuals. Basketball star Magic Johnson contracted the virus because he had unprotected sex with a woman who was HIV-positive. A baby can contract HIV from its mother. A woman can become infected if her sex partner is an intravenous drug user who has contracted the virus. Your sexual orientation does not determine whether or not you will contract HIV. Unfortunately, many people in our society still discriminate against homosexuals. Such people frequently discriminate against all people infected with HIV.

Although HIV and AIDS in America were originally associated with gay men, in other countries they are mainly associated with heterosexuals. In the United States today, the number of cases in the homosexual community is declining because of safer sex practices. Adolescents are now the group most likely to contract HIV, usually through heterosexual contact or intravenous drug use.

Being diagnosed HIV-positive is hard enough for a person to bear without having it complicated by judgments about one's private life.

Myth #8: AIDS is punishment for promiscuous behavior.

Reality: AIDS is the result of an infection, not a punishment. People who say that AIDS is a punishment are looking for an explanation for the unexplainable or looking to place blame. Some people also say that AIDS is punishment for homosexuality. The truth is that AIDS doesn't care if you're good or bad, or if you have sex with men or women, or if you have sex with ten people, one person, or no one. A person with AIDS is suffering from a physical problem, not a moral one.

Arthur Ashe, the famous tennis player, contracted AIDS through a blood transfusion. Ashe was known to be a kind, loving man. No one would say that he contracted AIDS as a punishment. Ryan White never had sexual intercourse with anyone; he learned he had AIDS when he was twelve years old. People who believe that AIDS is a punishment should ask themselves if people who contract the flu, chicken pox, or measles are being punished.

Myth #9: If you have HIV, it doesn't matter if you engage in risky behavior such as having unprotected sex or sharing intravenous drug works.

Reality: If you are HIV-positive, you have two major responsibilities: to take care of yourself, and to avoid infecting others. Being HIV-positive does not protect you from being reinfected. By engaging in unprotected sex or sharing drug paraphernalia you are taking the chance of contracting other diseases because your immune system has been weakened. You are also taking a chance of becoming infected with different strains of HIV. Doctors have identified different types of HIV; some are more aggressive than others. You are still at risk. Reinfection is one of the cofactors doctors believe that speeds up the growth of HIV.

Knowingly exposing others to HIV infection is a crime, both morally and legally. In many states, you can be prosecuted if you deliberately attempt to infect another person. If you are HIV-positive, you must use special care when having sexual intercourse to avoid reinfection and to avoid infecting your partner. You must tell your partner about your infection *before* you have intercourse.

If you are HIV-positive and are an intravenous drug user, you should think very seriously about stopping drug use. If you will not stop, do not share needles. Thoroughly clean needles or syringes with bleach and water. Understand that if you continue to use drugs, you are lessening your chances for survival.

If you have a friend who is HIV-positive and uses drugs, try to persuade him or her to seek counseling for help in getting off drugs.

Myth #10: A negative test result means that you do not have HIV.

Reality: A negative test result means that the antibodies for the virus did not appear on this test. It may take from six weeks to six months—and even up to a year—after exposure for the body to begin manufacturing the antibodies for HIV. The test can only determine if antibodies are present at that moment. If you have engaged in unsafe practices such as unprotected sexual intercourse or sharing drug paraphernalia, a negative HIV test may mean that you have not yet developed the antibodies for the virus. The time between exposure to HIV and the development of HIV antibodies is called "the window of opportunity." Although you may test negative for HIV, you may still be able to transmit the infection to others. If you have engaged in risky behavior and your HIV test says you are seronegative, you should consider being tested again in several months. But a negative test may mean just that—a negative test.

On the other hand, if your HIV test turns out positive, you should know that sometimes there are "false positives." If you have not engaged in risky behavior and you are given an ELISA test (Enzyme-linked Immunosorbent Assay), it is possible for it to read positive incorrectly. Ask your doctor if the Western Blot test was done to confirm the results of the ELISA test. In some states it is against the law to tell a patient about a positive ELISA test result before confirming the results by doing the Western Blot test.

Myth #11: If you are HIV-positive, you have no future.

Reality: Many people who have been diagnosed as HIV-positive go on to live long and productive lives. Some people who are HIV-positive do go on to develop AIDS, but many do not.

It is important to try to move forward. Doctors believe that stress and depression speed the breakdown of the immune system. They encourage their patients to remain active and involved in life. Whether an HIV-positive person will develop AIDS is not known. What is known and what is important is that a diagnosis of HIV does not mean that a person should stop living.

Magic Johnson learned he was HIV-positive in 1991. That diagnosis did not stop him from living. He continues to work as a sportscaster as well as a spokesperson for others who are similarly infected. Magic understands how important hope is when you are afflicted with a serious disease; he travels around the country encouraging people with HIV and AIDS.

A diagnosis of HIV can mean a new beginning if you are willing to take up the challenge. Thousands of people all over the world are living full lives even though they have HIV.

All of the above myths are dangerous and can come between people who are HIV-positive and people who are not. In order to better help someone who is HIV-positive, it is important to know what is true and what is not. In order to better help yourself if you are HIV-positive, it is important to know the difference between reality and myths.

CHAPTER 3

If You Think You May Be HIV-Positive

Getting an HIV test has become easier in recent years. More test facilities have been opened, and there are now tests that can be performed privately, at home. But being tested for HIV is still not a simple process for anyone. It is especially difficult for teens. First of all, you may not know what the tests are like or how to get one. Trying to keep the test a secret from your family and friends can put you under an extra and unnecessary emotional burden.

It is important to realize that the test is not an isolated event. It is only one in a series of steps that lead from your past to your future. If you test negative, you will probably need to take another test in a few months to confirm that you are free of the virus. You should also consider changing the behavior that put you at risk for HIV. If you test positive, you will need counseling to help you sort through your feelings and find medical treatment.

A good way to come to terms with your situation is to take a look at the entire test process. Write down these questions, think about them, then write down your answers.

- Why do you think you may be HIV-positive?
- Are you prepared to be tested for HIV?
- Are there any facilities or agencies near you that can help if you find out that you are HIV-positive?
- What is the standard testing procedure for HIV?
- Do you know about the new home tests for HIV?
- Should you take the standard test or a home test?
- Do you have a friend or trusted adult who will help you through the test process?
- What do the test results mean?

1. Why do you think you may be HIV-positive?

First, why do you want to be tested? You may have experienced some of the symptoms associated with HIV infection such as fatigue, rapid weight loss, diarrhea, shortness of breath, cough, nightsweats, chills, fever, thrush, swollen lymph nodes, or vision problems. But unless you can combine these symptoms with a source for contracting HIV, you are probably worrying needlessly. *It is not easy to get HIV.*

To determine if you have been exposed to a source of HIV infection, ask yourself the following questions:

Have you ever had a blood transfusion?
Before 1985, blood supplies were not routinely checked to see if they were contaminated with HIV. Since 1985, however, all blood in the United States as well as most other countries is checked to make certain that it is free of HIV. However, be aware that there is always a slim chance that a contaminated blood sample will be missed. A person cannot get

HIV by donating blood, only by receiving infected blood.

Have you used intravenous drugs or "skin-poppers"?
If you are an intravenous drug user, your chances of getting HIV are much higher than if you are not. Using intravenous drugs does not necessarily mean you will become HIV-positive, but if you use an unclean needle or share needles or syringes, your chances of becoming infected increase dramatically. HIV is carried in blood, and one of the quickest ways to introduce it into your system is to use a needle that has been used by someone who already has HIV. Skin-poppers are drugs that are injected into the skin, not the vein. When you skin-pop using a needle that may be contaminated, you are at serious risk for infection with HIV as well as other diseases.

Have you engaged in unprotected sexual intercourse?
If you have had sex without a condom, you increase your chances of contracting the virus. It doesn't matter whether you had sex with one person or ten people. Sex by itself does not cause infection, but sex with an infected person can pass the disease to you. You cannot contract HIV by touching or petting, but you *can* get it by having intercourse—either anal, vaginal, or oral—with an infected person, especially if you have an open cut or sore that comes in contact with the blood or semen of that person.

Have you been sexually abused by someone who is an intravenous drug user or is HIV-positive?
If your answer is yes, you are at multiple risk not only for contracting HIV but for the physical, psychologi-

cal, and emotional harm that afflicts victims of sexual abuse. In cases where sexual abuse is suspected, the courts may require a test for HIV.

Were either of your parents diagnosed as being HIV-positive when you were younger?
Men can pass the virus to women, who can then pass it to a fetus. Usually, HIV-positive babies are diagnosed at about six weeks. Some babies who test positive at birth can test negative several weeks later. If you are a teenager and neither of your parents were diagnosed as HIV-positive until recently, you probably did not contract the virus while you were a fetus. The fact that someone in your home is HIV-positive does not mean that you are infected as well. You cannot get HIV by sharing a home, a bathroom, a glass, or even a bed with someone who is infected. There must be an exchange of body fluids, such as having unprotected sex or sharing drug needles or syringes.

If you answered no to all of these questions, it is highly unlikely that you have been infected.

If you answered yes to one or more of these questions, you may have reason to be tested for HIV. But there are still many things to think about before you do.

2. Are you prepared to be tested for HIV?

Even if you have reason to believe you are infected, that does not necessarily mean that you should go ahead and be tested right away. Before anyone is tested for HIV, it is important to receive counseling from a qualified person. In the event you decide to take a home test, you should still receive pre-test counseling.

It is important to know beforehand if treatment programs are available for those who test positive. If facilities are not available for emotional counseling, as well as medical care, testing will serve only to upset you. This is a major problem for adolescents, because few centers are dedicated to helping teenagers who test HIV-positive. Many facilities are available for children under thirteen and adults over eighteen. Teenagers seem to be in limbo. Therefore, if you really want to be tested, you must check out the resources available in the event you test positive.

What if there are no resources available in your community? You can try approaching your family doctor. He or she can not only help you get tested but also direct you to the proper counseling services. Although doctors are supposed to respect the confidentiality of their patients, especially concerning sexually transmitted diseases, some doctors may feel compelled to tell your parents about your request. Be prepared for this to happen.

If you don't have a family doctor or don't feel comfortable with him or her, try calling the mental health clinic at any hospital. You can explain your problem without giving your name. You can also call the National AIDS hot line to find out which resources are close to you. The more you ask, the more information you will receive. It is just as important to know what you are going to do *after* you have been tested as it is to be tested.

Suppose you have reason to believe you may have been exposed to the virus and you want to be tested, but you don't want to tell anyone before you know for sure. Then you will have to think very carefully about the advantages of the new home tests and the standard test administered at medical facilities. Most states allow adolescents to be tested at a medical facility without the consent of a parent or guardian. The results are generally considered confidential, but there is no guarantee your parents or guardians or others will not be notified.

Your age is not a factor in the home tests. They allow you to remain anonymous and to control disclosure of the results. This makes home testing seem like a good choice for teenagers worried abut dealing with their families. But the test done at a medical facility has other advantages, including access to counseling before and after the test. You should not make a choice until you have compared the different tests and understand your options.

3. Do you know the standard way to test for HIV?
When HIV enters the body, the body produces antibodies in response to the virus. For several years the standard test for HIV has been a blood test that detects the presence of these antibodies in a small sample of your blood. To receive this test, you must go to a medical facility where a health-care worker draws about a teaspoon of your blood, usually from your arm. The blood is sent to a lab for screening. A procedure known as ELISA (Enzyme-linked Immunosorbent Assay) is applied. Another procedure, known as the Western Blot, is used to confirm the results of the ELISA. The test does not diagnose AIDS. It can only determine whether a person has HIV antibodies in his or her bloodstream.

Where can you get tested?
Most medical offices, hospitals, health departments, and family planning clinics offer testing for HIV. Clinics that specialize in treating sexually transmitted diseases also usually offer HIV testing. If your community has a high incidence of HIV infection, there may be special "alternative" sites or other programs

set up by the health department or interested community organizations. Alternative sites are places to go for testing without passersby knowing where you are going. Not all places in a community offer the same services or prices. Shop around. If you have difficulty locating a place to take the test, get more information by calling one of the toll-free hot lines listed at the end of this book.

How much will it cost?
Your local health department probably offers the test free. Private testing sites have been known to charge up to $80 for an HIV antibody test. Don't feel shy about asking about cost. You are a consumer, and the testing places are offering a service.

Do I need permission from my parents or guardians to get tested?
Generally not. Most states allow teenagers to consent to testing for sexually transmitted or contagious diseases. In many areas HIV qualifies as a sexually transmitted or contagious disease.

How long will it take to get the results?
Test results are generally available in about two weeks.

How will you get the results of the test?
There are many different ways. Each testing site has its own preferred method. Some sites will send your results by mail, others will inform you by phone, and still others will request that you return to the testing site. In most cases, the best solution is to go back to the testing site. This not only eliminates the

possibility of someone accidentally learning the results, it also allows a counselor to evaluate your response and offer you guidance and support. A testing site that offers counseling before and after testing is preferable. Also, places that offer follow-up medical care and psychological support are preferable to those that do not. Your area may not have all of these services available. While that does limit your possibilities, it does not limit your right to information.

No matter where you choose to go, make a list of questions you want to ask. Take the list with you and ask the questions one by one. Check off each one as it is answered to your understanding. The only stupid question is the one you don't ask.

4. What is the new home test for HIV?

Kits for self-administered HIV testing are now available under two brand names, Confide and Home Access. Like the standard test, the home test detects the presence of HIV antibodies in the blood. Each home test kit includes complete directions, a small lancet, a piece of filter paper, a 3-digit ID code, and a mailing envelope. You use the lancet to prick your finger and release a few drops of blood on the filter paper. You then put the filter paper in the envelope and mail it to a lab for processing. You keep the 3-digit ID number. It is the only way your blood sample will be identified at the manufacturer's lab.

Where can you buy a home test?
Kits for home testing are available at pharmacies, mass merchandise outlets, clinics, college health centers, and by direct mail order from the manufacturer.

How much will a home test kit cost?
On average $50.

Is sale of the home test kits regulated?
You do not need a doctor's prescription to buy a home test kit, nor do you need to show proof of age. Anyone can buy a home test kit.

How long will it take to get the results of the test?
The results will be available in about a week.

How do you get the results of the test?
By telephoning a toll-free number listed in the kit and stating your 3-digit ID code. A pre-recorded message reports negative results. Positive results are explained by a counselor who will also refer you to health-care facilities in your area. As in the case of the standard HIV test, you should have a written list of questions to ask the counselor.

5. Should you get the standard test or a home test?

The home tests have the advantage of convenience, privacy, and speed. However, many health-care providers have voiced concern over several aspects of the home tests. They worry that the blood sample will be contaminated before it reaches the lab and thus give inaccurate results. They also fear that people will start to use them as a "morning after" check that allows them to continue reckless behavior. They also question the quality of the telephone counseling provided by the manufacturers of the kits.

Advocates of home testing argue that the tests are accurate and that the counseling is thorough and sensitive.

They also claim that the home tests will help slow the spread of HIV among adolescents. Studies have shown that teenagers are reluctant to undergo testing and often wait until they are HIV-symptomatic. This may not happen until they reach their twenties, after years of infection and experimentation with sex and drugs. Advocates of home testing think the new tests will encourage young people to get tested before they become HIV-symptomatic. If they test positive, they will be able to start early treatment and delay the onset of AIDS. And knowing that they are HIV-positive will force them to take steps to protect their sexual partners from the disease.

Another factor to take into account is your financial situation. The standard test can generally be arranged free of cost, and it will be accompanied by face-to-face counseling. A home test costs around $50, and you will have to rely on a telephone conversation for counseling if you test positive. You should also keep in mind that other tests are available. A test using fluids from inside the mouth has been approved for routine use.

6. Is there a friend or trusted adult who will help you through the test process?

An HIV test is a frightening event. It can be even more terrifying if you are alone with your fear. Although your first reaction may be to keep the whole process a secret, you need to think about that again. Keeping a secret like HIV to yourself can be a great burden. Some testing sites actually request that you bring someone with you because getting a positive diagnosis can be a serious shock. You should keep this in mind if you decide to use a home test. Find someone you trust to provide support and guidance at every step of the way.

7. What do the results of the tests mean?

If your test result is negative, it means no antibodies for HIV were in your system at the moment your blood was drawn. There is a "window of opportunity" between the time of infection and the development of HIV antibodies. During this period, tests for HIV will be negative. If your test result is negative, think again about why you thought you needed to be tested. You may need to be retested in several months. If the test is a true negative test, that does not mean you should go back to "life as usual." If you thought you had been exposed through risky behavior such as unprotected sex or intravenous drug use, you need to protect yourself against future worry. You must actively work to change your habits. Only you can protect yourself against the virus.

If your result is positive, there is a slight chance that it may be false positive and that a second test will prove negative. If you are diagnosed as HIV-positive you have a lot to think about and a lot to do. The next few chapters discuss coping with a positive diagnosis.

CHAPTER 4

Testing Positive: What Now?

If your test result was positive, it is natural to experience many conflicting emotions. Some of the more common ones are anger, guilt, shame, fear, and depression. Different people will experience different emotions, and different people will experience the same emotions differently. Because the immune system responds negatively to stress, it is very important for you to learn strategies to cope with these emotions. You may have all of these feelings, some of these feelings, or other feelings entirely. There is no order in which you should feel these emotions. You need to be able to recognize them in order to learn to deal with them constructively. It is also important for those around you to understand their emotions and learn how to cope with them. HIV affects not only the person who is infected but everyone who loves and cares for that person.

COPING WITH ANGER

Anger is a common response to bad news, especially bad news over which you have no control. People also become angry when they think something is unfair. Contracting HIV when you are young seems unfair. Anger at a diagnosis of HIV-positive is an understandable response. But you need to express your anger appropriately and direct it responsibly.

Jerry's Story

When Jerry found out he was HIV-positive, he was very angry. He was sixteen years old and had tried intravenous drugs when he was thirteen. He had done it only a few times at parties, and everyone had shared the same needle. He thought he knew the night when he was probably infected. An older guy, Rick, was at the party, and it seemed to Jerry that he knew a lot about drugs. Jerry guessed that he had contracted HIV after sharing a needle with Rick. He was angry because that night he really hadn't wanted to get high. But he wanted Rick to think he was cool, so he went along.

"I was really mad," Jerry says. "I stayed in my room for two weeks without talking to anyone, except to tell my mom to shut up and get away from my door. I broke everything in my room. I guess my mom thought I was going crazy. I hadn't told her about experimenting with drugs, and now I was going to have to live with that mistake for the rest of my life. Mom would put food outside the door, and I'd just throw it down the hall and scream at her to mind her own business. I don't know how she survived it.

Finally, I realized that I needed to pull myself together, that I wasn't solving anything with that kind of anger. I knew I had to tell Mom what was going on if I wanted to ever feel normal again."

Jerry's anger at contracting HIV was normal and understandable. But his anger toward his mother, the food, and the things in his room was misdirected. He was really angry at the disease.

We often lash out at those around us when we are angry. It doesn't mean that we don't love them or that we blame them for what has happened. It simply means that we are angry and don't know what to do. Anger becomes a problem if it remains misdirected. If Jerry had continued to yell at his mother, she probably would have become angry at him. She might then have reacted by shouting back at him or even calling the police.

If you were a friend of Jerry's and he behaved to you the way he did to his mother, what would you have done?

What would have happened if Jerry's mother had gotten angry at him? Do you think Jerry would have responded by getting even angrier? How could Jerry have handled this situation differently?

If both Jerry and his mother had misdirected their anger, it would have been very difficult for either of them to express their real feelings and to keep their home a safe emotional place.

If you have learned that you are HIV-positive and you are angry, think carefully about how you express that anger. Destroying property or hurting others is not a healthy expression of anger. You are angry at the disease, not at your friends or family. It is up to you to channel your anger in a way that is beneficial to you. Some people exercise to get rid of anger. Some people join HIV support groups and talk their anger out with others. Some consult a therapist to learn other ways to cope with their anger.

If you are HIV-positive and are unable to tell a trusted friend or family member about it, you may become even angrier than the person who shares the diagnosis with a loving person. If you have not told anyone about your diagnosis, maybe you need to rethink that decision. Keeping the diagnosis all to yourself can be a heavy burden. If the people who love you are aware of your problem, they may be better able to cope with your anger and to help you redirect it in a more constructive manner.

If Jerry's mother had known that he had tested positive for HIV, she might have handled the situation differently. When Jerry shouted at her, she would have known that he was angry at the disease, not at her. She would have been able to tell him that he had every right to be angry and that she was on his side. When you are angry, it is important to have others acknowledge that you have a reason to be angry. If others do not know why you are angry, and shouting, they are likely to assume that your anger is personal. Then everyone is likely to be angry at everyone else, when the real villain is HIV.

If you have a friend who is HIV-positive, you need to try to understand your friend's anger and even understand that sometimes it will be misdirected at you.

Shantay and Lisa

Shantay and Lisa had been friends ever since first grade. They had drifted apart when Lisa started dating Alex because Shantay didn't get along with him. Lisa learned she might be HIV-positive after Alex told her that he had tested positive. Alex was an intravenous drug user who probably contracted the virus from sharing needles. Shantay went with Lisa when Lisa went to be tested and again to get the result, which was positive. The first few days Lisa was very quiet. She and Shantay just hung around doing nothing special and not talking about Lisa's diagnosis. But one day while they were watching TV, Lisa turned to Shantay and said angrily,

"I bet you're glad this happened. You probably think I deserve it. You never liked Alex, anyway."

Before Shantay could answer. Lisa stormed out of the room. Shantay was shocked at Lisa's anger. When she tried to call her the next day, Lisa hung up on her. She waited a few more days and tried again, but Lisa still refused to talk to her. Eventually Shantay just stopped trying to get in touch with Lisa.

What would you have done if you were Shantay? Lisa was angry because she had learned she was HIV-positive, not because of anything Shantay had done. Lisa made it difficult because she would not answer Shantay's phone calls. Because Lisa misdirected her anger at Shantay, Shantay stopped trying to be friends with her.

Can you think of another way Shantay could have dealt with Lisa besides just not bothering anymore? She could have written Lisa a letter:

Dear Lisa,
I am very sorry that you are sick and I am trying to understand how you feel. I know it's not fair and that you must

feel very angry right now. I wish there was a way to change all of this. Lisa, I need to say that my feelings were hurt when you said I was probably glad you were sick. I know that was just your anger, but it still was hurtful. I am still your friend, but I don't want to intrude. Please let me know what I can do to make things easier for you. Love, Shantay

Shantay acknowledged Lisa's right to be angry but at the same time let her know how she felt. She didn't say, "You hurt my feelings." Instead she wrote, "My feelings were hurt." When you are dealing with someone who is very angry, it makes matters worse if you sound accusing. Try to avoid "You" statements; use "I" statements instead.

There are things that you can do to help your friend redirect his or her anger in a more constructive manner. However, you do have a right to speak up. No one likes to be subjected to verbal abuse, no matter what the reason. At the same time, you need to be careful how you respond to misdirected anger.

What if Shantay had actually believed that Lisa was partly at fault for dating Alex and said so? People who become infected are often blamed for contracting the disease. Even if you do secretly believe this, you need to remember that no one deserves to be sick and that no one has sex or uses drugs with the intention of contracting HIV. Ask yourself if you blamed Ryan White for contracting AIDS, or if you think rock star Freddie Mercury deserved to die from AIDS. Do you think a teenager should die just because he or she was driving too fast trying to get home by curfew? If you think about these things and still believe that your friend is responsible for his or her illness, *keep it to yourself*. Expressing the feeling will certainly be no help to your friend and will only demonstrate your lack of knowledge about HIV.

Sometimes when a person is diagnosed with HIV, the anger may become so great that he or she tries to hurt others.

Saundra's Story

Saundra was fifteen when she ran away from home to escape a father who sexually abused her. She made her way to Detroit, where she met up with some other runaway teenagers. They all slept in the basement of an abandoned building.

Like many other runaways, Saundra had no skills that she could use to support herself, so she became a prostitute. She didn't know what else to do, but she became very depressed about her life. She began taking drugs, at first just pills, but soon she was shooting up heroin. When Saundra was high, nothing bothered her. She and her friends frequently shared needles and drugs.

One day when Saundra needed money badly, she decided to give blood. At the blood bank, she had to fill out a form giving her name and address. She gave her first name but made up a last name, and she used the address of a bar where she sometimes hung out. When she had given the blood, Saundra was paid. She took the money and bought her drugs.

A couple of weeks later, Saundra was in the bar, and one of the bartenders handed her an envelope.

"This you?" he asked.

Saundra recognized the name she had given to the blood bank and took the envelope. The letter inside was brief; it said that when screening her blood for HIV the test had come up positive, and it suggested that she consult a doctor immediately.

After the initial shock wore off, Saundra became very angry. After all, she had done nothing bad to anyone. She was only trying to survive. Why did this have to happen to her? She began looking for someone to blame. She felt that none of this would ever have happened to her if her father had just left her alone. And Saundra was sure that one of the men who had paid her for sex had given her HIV.

Because she couldn't get even with her father, Saundra decided to get even with any man she could. Even though she knew that one of the easiest ways to spread HIV is through unprotected intercourse, she continued to have sex without using condoms. She never told any of her partners that she was infected. She justified this to herself by saying that if these men were willing to have sex with a girl young enough to be their daughter, they deserved anything they got.

Can you understand why Saundra was so angry? Life had been unfair to her, but the way Saundra handled her anger was unfair to many other innocent people. She never even stopped to consider that she might have contracted HIV from sharing needles with her friends. She was striking out because of all the bad things that had happened to her. Saundra did not deserve to contract HIV, but neither did the men with whom she had sex.

The problem with anger such as Saundra's is that it can kill other people. The men whom she might have infected could have gone home and unknowingly exposed their wives or any number of other people. Although you may think as Saundra did—that the men deserved what they got—ask yourself if the people these men may have infected also deserved to get HIV.

HIV is not a punishment; it is a disease. It does not single out bad people over good. HIV does not discriminate.

What Saundra did was illegal. If you are HIV-positive and have been thinking of venting your anger as Saundra did, you need to think again. You contracted HIV because you were exposed to someone who already had the virus, so the person who gave it to you is probably already suffering. Why would you want to infect someone else? If you have a friend who is HIV-positive and is planning to infect someone on purpose, you have a responsibility to try to stop it. Your friend is committing a crime.

COPING WITH GUILT AND SHAME

Guilt and shame are also common reactions to receiving a positive diagnosis. One reason for these emotions is that many people remain uneducated about HIV and view it as an expected result of promiscuity, gay sex, or drug abuse. The truth is that people do not expect to contract HIV, and that is why they do not take precautions. They are not thinking about HIV, but about the experience.

Marshall's Story

When sixteen-year-old Marshall found out he was HIV-positive, he felt ashamed. He didn't know how he was going to tell his parents. He knew they would ask how he had become infected, and he did not want to tell them. Marshall had been involved in a homosexual relationship for over a year. He had worked very hard to keep his parents from knowing he was gay. Now that he was infected with HIV, he felt he was being punished for being gay.

"I didn't know what to do at first. I felt I had let my mother down. I didn't think I could face her. And my father! There was no way he was going to understand."

Marshall had confided in his counselor at the testing center. He told her he thought he had contracted the virus during homosexual intercourse. She gave him the number of a gay crisis center, and he made an appointment there. Although no one could tell Marshall's parents for him, the people at the crisis center gave him tips on what to say and how to respond when he told his parents. They also encouraged Marshall to join a support group, which he did.

Marshall's parents were shocked, confused, and angry when he first told them that he was gay and HIV-positive. With the help of a support group for parents of gay children, they learned more about homosexuality. The more they learned, the easier it was for them to accept Marshall as the person he always had been and to give him their full love and support. Marshall learned to get over his feelings of guilt and shame and to go on with his life.

Because some people in our society are misinformed about homosexuality and consider it wrong, a person who contracts HIV through homosexual sex may receive less sympathy than someone who contracted it another way. This is even more difficult for a teenager whose parents or friends are unaware of his or her sexual orientation. Before Marshall's parents went to counseling, they were under the false impression that Marshall was gay because of something they had or had not done. The truth is, people do not *choose* their sexual orientation. Sexual orientation is neither good nor bad. It is just part of who a person is. And although people can choose whom they have sex with, they have no way of being sure whether their partner is infected with HIV.

If you were Marshall's friend and he talked to you about feeling guilty, what would you say to him? You could tell him that you understand why he might feel guilty, but that he really had no reason to do so. You could also tell him that guilt is not very productive, that it doesn't change the past or the diagnosis.

Suppose you had not known Marshall was gay. How would you have reacted when he told you? Would you have pulled away when you were told? Would you have worried that Marshall was trying to recruit you to a homosexual lifestyle? Remember that sexual orientation is not something one chooses; it is something that each of us is born with. If Marshall had been sexually interested in you, you probably would have had some sign of it earlier. Sharing a secret like homosexuality means that you trust the person not to turn away.

The important thing in Marshall's case is not his sexual orientation but the fact that he is infected with HIV, and scared. If you were his friend, you would hug him or touch his hand and let him know you were a true friend who knew the facts about sexual orientation and HIV.

If you have HIV and feel ashamed or guilty, take some time to think about yourself. Make a list of all the things you can do. Make another list of all your good qualities. Think about who your friends are and why you like them. You may find that you have many of the qualities that you like about them, and that is why you are friends. Think about something good that you have done. Then think about another good thing you have done. Stop focusing on how you got the disease; you cannot change the past. The only bad thing someone does is to hurt another person deliberately. Forgive yourself. You did nothing mean, evil, or bad.

If you cannot stop feeling guilty or ashamed, you probably ought to talk to someone about it. HIV counselors could help you stop misdirecting your anger at yourself and help you to move forward. Feeling guilty or ashamed wastes your emotional energy and adds to your stress. There are real and positive things that you need to be doing right now, such as taking care of yourself both physically and emotionally. Allow yourself the same compassion and understanding you would give to someone else.

COPING WITH FEAR

There are several different fears that a person diagnosed with HIV might experience: fear of death, fear of sickness, fear of losing family or friends, fear of passing the virus on to someone else. If you are afraid of something, the first thing you need to do is get more information about it. People tend to fear what they do not know.

Bertha's Story

When Bertha learned she was HIV-positive, she felt as if her life were over. She believed that she would die at any moment. Every night she went to bed expecting not to wake up in the morning. And every morning she woke up surprised to be there. She refused to leave the house for fear she might get sick away from home. She stopped talking to her friends and wouldn't go to school. It wasn't long before Bertha *was* sick, but not from HIV. She was sick from anxiety, stress, and lack of sleep.

HIV is not a death sentence. Bertha's fear, while understandable, was unreasonable. Many people who are HIV-positive go on to live productive, happy lives. It is one thing to be afraid of dying or being sick, but it is another to become obsessed with it.

Most of us, at one time or another, are afraid of death or dying. Usually we come to accept that death is something that happens to us all, and when we reach that conclusion we can go on living our lives. Few people know how much time they have to live. Having HIV does not change that. Being HIV-positive may mean that you will develop AIDS and may very well die from it. But then again, you may not.

Fear of death is an emotion much like guilt or shame: It serves no useful purpose. There's nothing you can do about it. You don't know when death will come. But you do know that the stress caused by worrying can diminish the effectiveness of the immune system and cause you to become sicker earlier.

Some people say it's not death they fear, but the process of dying. But worrying about death or dying won't prevent it. The more you know about something, the less you will fear it. Many books on death and dying are available. More important, there are also many books on living with HIV. Some are listed in the back of this book. Your school librarian or counselor can help you find even more. Every day, new information becomes available to help those who have HIV live better and longer lives.

Because being HIV-positive makes a person more susceptible to a variety of infections, it is not unusual to fear sickness. There are things you can do to keep this fear in check. First of all, keep yourself informed. Having HIV doesn't mean that every time you catch a cold or throw up, you have AIDS. Don't panic every time you feel sick. Ask your doctor which symptoms are important to report and which are not. Take care of your body. If you cannot control the fear, you probably ought to see a counselor. Sometimes the only way to get rid of it is to have a professional person help you talk through it. A person who is excessively fearful of being sick may really be afraid of dying. Talking about these feelings with a trusted adult or friend can help put your mind at ease.

If you have a friend who is HIV-positive, neither dismiss nor affirm his or her fears about being sick. You can be of more help to your friend if you know something about HIV and its symptoms. Read up on it.

If you are HIV-positive and are afraid of losing your family or friends, you need to confront those feelings. If you are keeping silent about your illness because you are afraid of losing certain relationships, ask yourself whether keeping quiet makes you less afraid. It is possible that it may actually make you more fearful as you constantly struggle to keep others from knowing. The truth is that some people will reject you, but others will not. If you join an HIV support group, other group members can help you sort out your feelings about whom to tell and whom not to tell. A support group offers a safe place to express your fears because someone else in the group is bound to have had similar feelings.

If you are HIV-positive, it will be difficult to keep the knowledge from your parents or guardians. Usually they are the ones who must assume the responsibility for your medical treatment. If you do not tell them, and therefore do not get medical treatment, you are putting yourself in serious danger. At least give them the opportunity to respond for your own well-being. Although many parents may respond with anger at first, just as many will respond with love and understanding from the start.

Unfortunately, discrimination is a way of life for many people with HIV, and some people will reject you. While it may be true that you are better off without those people, that doesn't make it feel any better. Sometimes we like people we know we shouldn't like—there's no explaining it. Remember, you have the right to decide whom you want to tell. You are not required to tell anyone except your doctor, your dentist, and anyone you may have exposed to the virus.

When some people are first diagnosed with HIV, they become so afraid of passing the virus on to others that they shy away from any sort of touching. The solution to this fear is information. HIV is not passed on through casual contact. You cannot "give" HIV to someone by sharing the same room, the same bed, or the same bathroom or water glass. You cannot "give" someone HIV by kissing or holding hands. HIV is spread by sharing body fluids such as blood and semen. You can spread HIV by having unprotected sex or by sharing needles. It is a lot easier for you to catch something from someone else than it is for that person to "contract" HIV from you. HIV is not easy to get. If you have been avoiding people you love for fear of giving them the virus, you have been depriving yourself of their company and the comfort they could give.

Micah's Story

Micah was surprised when he learned he was HIV-positive. Although he had been having unprotected sex for three years, since he was twelve years old, he had never thought about getting HIV. He had run away from home a couple of weeks before his twelfth birthday and lived on the street for two years until he got up the courage to go home. He had kept himself alive those two years as a male prostitute.

Micah's parents were supportive of him when he first came home. The whole family went to counseling to learn how to deal with their problems in constructive ways. The counselor suggested that Micah be tested for HIV. When Micah tested positive, his parents were embarrassed and stopped going to counseling. Although they said they wanted to understand what was happening to their son, by not continuing to see the counselor they lost an important resource for comfort and information. There was much that Micah and his parents did not know about HIV, and that lack of knowledge made life more difficult for everyone. Micah felt that he was a danger to his family, and the little things his parents did only increased his worries. His mother was always spraying the mouthpiece of the telephone with disinfectant after Micah had used it, and his father stopped using the bathroom downstairs near Micah's bedroom. Micah became extra cautious with his family. When his mother came near him, he would move away. He stopped seeing his friends because he was afraid he might infect them too.

Micah's life became unnecessarily lonely, as did the lives of his parents and friends who had enjoyed his company. If Micah's parents had taken the time to get more information, they would have known that they could not "catch" the virus from their son. All the precautions that they took were not only unnecessary, but also very hurtful for Micah. Just when he needed the love and support of family and friends, Micah's parents made him fearful and isolated.

It is not unusual for someone who has tested positive for HIV to start imagining all sorts of illnesses and to go out of the way to avoid touching others for fear of contaminating them. If you have a friend who is HIV-positive, be aware of how you act. Do you avoid touching something your friend has touched? Do you sit farther away than you used to? Have you stopped hugging your friend? If you answered yes to any of these questions, you are probably causing your friend a lot of pain. While it is important to take care of yourself, that does not mean that you have the right to do so at the expense of someone else. If you are afraid to be around someone who is HIV-positive even after you know the facts, you need to keep your prejudice to yourself. In fact, the person may need you to hug and hold him or her more than ever. The human touch is a wonderful gift for anyone who is afraid. Make an extra effort to show your friend that you are comfortable being with him or her.

COPING WITH DEPRESSION

Depression occurs when someone loses hope. When people are depressed they tend to think a lot about death and dying. Sometimes they think about suicide. Being diagnosed with HIV can be a depressing experience. People often feel helpless as well as hopeless. That is why almost all HIV testing centers provide counseling for patients who have tested positive. Depression is a reasonable response to a diagnosis of HIV. A person who is depressed often feels tired and sad all the time. He or she may sleep a lot but never feel rested. If you are experiencing any of these symptoms or have stopped seeing your friends or doing things that you used to enjoy, you may be depressed.

Having HIV does not mean that your life is over or that you have no future. Although there is not yet a cure for HIV, new methods for treating the disease have been developed during the past few years. The new treatments have reversed the progress of the disease in thousands of patients, and there is every likelihood that further advances in treatment are on the way. Although you cannot control the course of HIV, you can take control of your life by understanding how HIV works, what it does, and what you can do to protect yourself against infections. By taking control, the feeling of helplessness disappears and so does the feeling of hopelessness.

Marianne's Story

When Marianne first learned she was HIV-positive, she became very depressed. She had contracted the virus from her boyfriend, Bernard, who had become infected after having sex once with a girl he met at a bar. At first Marianne cried every day: Here she was, seventeen years old, and her life was over. She would never go to college, never get married, never have a child, a home of her own, a career. Everything she had ever dreamed of vanished in the moment she received the HIV test result. Finally, her mother took her to see a counselor, Dr. Hamrick, who specialized in treating teenagers with HIV.

The doctor told Marianne that she had every right to be sad and angry, and whatever else she felt. But he also told her that she was not dead yet, and that if she wanted anything out of life she had to get started on it now. One of the first things she could do, he said, was to learn about HIV. If Marianne was well informed, she would be able to take control of her life even if she couldn't control her illness. Dr. Hamrick told Marianne about a support group for teens with HIV.

The first time Marianne went to the support group meeting, she was very surprised at the teenagers she met there. They were all about the same age, but some were very sick while others looked as if they had never been ill. But all of them eagerly welcomed Marianne and began to tell her about their experiences. By the time Marianne met with the group for the third session, she felt very different. She had come to realize that life was over only when you said it was over. Her new friends had given her the hope and the courage she needed to face the future, sick or well.

When you are depressed, it isn't always easy to know what to do. Sometimes talking with others in the same situation can be helpful. Studies have shown that cancer patients who join support groups tend to live longer than those who don't. One reason may be that in a support group you can explore feelings that are familiar to others. You also gain access to the information others have gotten through their experiences. Members of support groups help each other through the bad times and share the good times. It is often hard to explain your problems to someone who doesn't have them. Having someone who already knows what you are talking about and going through makes it easier to express your feelings.

If you are depressed, tell your doctor. Sometimes a medication you are taking for HIV may cause depression. If this is so, your doctor can change the medication. Also, your doctor may be able to prescribe medication to alleviate the depression if it lingers.

You can also help ease depression by keeping your mind occupied. Read a book, go to a movie, play cards with friends, meditate, exercise. Remember, exercise releases endorphins, which nourish a sense of well-being.

If your depression lingers no matter what you do, you probably need to see a professional counselor. Your doctor, a mental health clinic, or someone in an HIV support group can recommend one. Depression causes stress, and too much stress is harmful to the immune system. Depression can also make you very tired, which in turn can increase the depression.

If you have a friend who is HIV-positive and is talking about suicide, you can help by spending time with him or her. Go to the movies or just out for a walk. Talk to your friend and try to see that he or she gets help to break out of the depression.

No one can predict what emotions a person will experience when faced with a diagnosis of HIV. This chapter touches on only some. You may experience all of them, some of them, or none of them. No matter what, the best way to help yourself is to get informed. Understand HIV and how it works. Know the difference between the myths and the facts.

The same is true if you have a friend who is HIV-positive. Find out about HIV. Understand the difference between HIV and AIDS. Listen when your friend wants to talk. Be open to hearing what he or she has to say, even if you find it uncomfortable. And—very important—give your friend a hug now and then. Show that you care.

CHAPTER 5

Commonly Asked Questions About Being HIV-Positive

Can HIV Be Cured?

Right now there is no cure for HIV. However, with new developments, it is on its way to being considered a "chronic management illness." If you take care of yourself, avoid stress as much as possible, and receive proper medical attention, you have a good chance of keeping the disease under control.

How Does It Feel to Have HIV?

When someone first contracts HIV, he or she may experience flu-like symptoms such as chills, fever, nightsweats, and diarrhea. Chances are, the person will not associate these with HIV. (If you have had these symptoms, *unless* you have engaged in risky behavior, don't worry.) After this initial reaction, an infected person may feel no symptoms for years. In fact, people infected with HIV are often unaware that they have the disease until they are tested for it.

Will I Get AIDS?

There is no way of telling whether you will develop AIDS. Many HIV-positive people never contract any of the diseases associated with AIDS; others do. The best thing to do is to get up-to-date medical treatment and avoid stress. At the tenth International Conference on AIDS in August 1994, scientists reported on research among people who had remained asymptomatic for more than twelve years. The only similarity they found among all of these people was their positive attitude towards the disease.

Can I Have Sexual Intercourse?

Having HIV does not mean that you cannot have sexual intercourse. It does mean that you cannot have unprotected intercourse without great risk to both you and your partner. Practicing "safe" sex has certain conditions. Your partner must be told that you are HIV-positive. If you do not do so, you are not giving your partner a fair chance, and you may be breaking the law. Some states have passed legislation that obligates HIV-positive people to inform anyone they have or will put at risk for the disease. You should never have any kind of sex—oral, anal, or vaginal—without a latex condom.

Latex is nonporous, which means that most of the time, body fluids will not escape or penetrate it. Condoms made of sheepskin or other animal skin are porous and do not prevent the exchange of body fluids. Also, remember that condoms are not perfect; they can break. The only certain way to completely avoid transmitting or contracting HIV is not to have sex.

Can I Get Married?

Of course, you can get married. Having HIV does not mean all other parts of your life must end. There are many marriages in which one or both partners have HIV. Magic Johnson is an example. When people love each other and want to be together, HIV does not need to stand in the way. However, it is essential to tell your partner about your illness *before* you make such an important decision. Your partner has a right to know, and marriage is supposed to be a sharing experience for both people. If you keep HIV a secret, you are not only harming your partner and breaking the law; you are also depriving yourself of the chance to have a full, open relationship with someone who loves you.

Can I Have Children?

If you are female and HIV-positive, there is some risk that you may pass the virus on to the fetus before, during, or after birth. It is also possible, however, that you will give birth to a healthy baby. All babies born to HIV-positive mothers inherit the mother's immune system; that means that they will test positive at birth. It takes about eighteen months to two years for a baby to develop its own immune system. After that time, about 25 percent of these babies remain infected and continue to test positive for HIV. Babies who remain HIV-positive generally die within a few years. Recent studies have shown that if an expectant mother who is HIV-positive takes AZT (a commonly pre-scribed drug for HIV), the chances of passing the virus to the baby during birth are reduced.

There is also a risk that an HIV-positive mother can pass the virus to her baby through breast-feeding. Breast milk is one of the body fluids that can carry HIV.

Another risk of pregnancy if you are HIV-positive is that the pregnancy may cause the virus to develop faster. This can cause your immune system to weaken more quickly at a time when your body needs to be at its strongest, putting you and the baby at serious risk. Talk to your doctor about your special circumstances. It may be that you place your life in danger if you have a baby right now. Your doctor may suggest other options.

In order to get pregnant, you and your partner will have to engage in unprotected intercourse. If you are female, HIV is found in vaginal secretions, and engaging in unpro-tected sexual intercourse increases the risk of infecting your partner.

If you are male and HIV-positive, you know that having unprotected sex will increase your partner's chances of contracting the virus. Semen is one of the body fluids that carries HIV. If you are thinking about having a baby, you both need to be fully aware of the risks.

Finally, if you know you are HIV-positive and decide to have a child, you need to think what will happen to that child if you or your partner should get sick. Many parents who have been diagnosed with AIDS are having to decide who will care for their children after they die. If you are HIV-positive, you need to consider seriously what will happen to your child if you develop AIDS.

Will I Be Able to Get a Job?

The only time you are obligated to disclose your HIV status to an employer is if you are trying to get a job in a health-care or health-care-related industry. It will probably be hard to get such a job once you have been diagnosed, although you won't be told that is the reason. The medical establishment is just as prone to prejudice and ignorance as any other business. If you really want a job related to health care, try someplace that is sympathetic to persons who have HIV or AIDS. The higher the incidence of HIV or AIDS in your community, the greater your chance of being hired.

Any prospective employer can request your medical records, but they cannot be released unless you agree. An employer cannot make seeing your medical records a condition of your employment. You are only required to reveal your status if you are a health-care worker.

Will People Be Able to Tell I Have HIV?

No visual signs accompany HIV infection. Some people look sick, some people look healthy, just like people without HIV. The only way a person will know you have HIV is if you tell them.

Should I Tell My Friends?

That is a hard one. It depends. . . . On one hand, if you really care for your friend you won't want to have a secret between you. The other possibility is that sometimes we like people who really are not our friends, that sometimes relationships are based on other things than true caring. Both sides are right. It is a decision only you can make. You may want to ask the advice of a counselor or another trusted adult before you tell any of your friends.

Should I Tell My Parents?

You don't have much choice. How can you get the medical care you need if you don't tell your parents? Telling your parents will probably be the hardest thing you have to do after you learn you are HIV-positive. The next chapter deals with the subject. Read it carefully. It may give you some ideas.

CHAPTER 6

Telling Your Parents

Telling your parents or guardians that you are HIV-positive may be one of the hardest things you will ever have to do, but it is also one of the most important. The laws in your state may allow you to be tested for HIV without your parents' consent but probably don't allow you to receive medical treatment without their permission. And even if your state does allow it, your parents are almost sure to be obligated to pay for it. So one reason you need to tell your parents is that they will have to pay for your treatment, and your health may depend on such treatment.

A second reason to tell your parents is that the burden of keeping such an enormous secret from people you live with may be more than you can handle. Such stress can further weaken your immune system and cause you to get sick. In addition, if you experience strong emotions such as anger, sadness, or depression, you will need your parents to give you the necessary care and affection.

Another reason to tell your parents is a very basic one: You are all part of a family, and one of the purposes of a family is to provide love, nurturing, and support.

HOW TO TELL YOUR PARENTS

If you are using drugs or having sex, your parents are likely to be aware of your activities even if they have not said so. Many parents are reluctant to discuss sexuality or even drug abuse with their children. That doesn't mean they don't love you; it just means they don't know how to talk to you about intimate subjects. If this is the case in your home, one thing you can do is to leave information about AIDS and HIV around the house. Your parents may gather that you are leaving a clue for them. If they fail to respond to your hints, you may have to be the one to initiate the discussion about HIV.

It will help to think out in advance what you are going to say. Putting it on paper is a good way to get started. Practice what you want to say out loud, with a trusted friend as an audience or just alone in your room. Practicing will make it easier to say the words, even if it doesn't make the situation any easier.

Think about what you need to say:

1. You want to tell them that you were tested and that you are HIV-positive.
2. You want to tell them when you were tested.
3. You may or may not want to tell them right away *why* you were tested, but that is something they will want to know.

    No matter how you contracted the virus, it will be hard to tell your parents. It may be especially difficult if you are a gay teenager and have never talked to your parents about your homosexuality.
4. Most important, you want to tell your parents that you are scared and that you need their love, help, and understanding.

If you tell your parents right away that you are scared, it may remind them that you are talking about having a disease, not about violating a curfew. That is important for everyone to remember. Having HIV is not about disobeying your parents. It is not something that can be cured by being grounded for a couple of months. Of course, if you could go back in time and change things, you would. But you can't, and you know that blaming yourself or feeling guilty only adds to unhealthy stress. Remind your parents that you cannot go back, that you need to think about how you are going to go forward.

It is also important to tell your parents what you expect from them: love, help, and understanding. It may help them to remember that families are supposed to stand together in bad times as well as good.

Try not to be defensive with your parents. It is all too easy to blame others for our own mistakes. Don't say things like, "If you had paid more attention to me, I would have been home more often," or "It's your fault that I took drugs because life was so miserable here." There may be some truth in those statements, but they serve no purpose here. If your parents sense that you are blaming them for your situation, their initial response may be defensive as well.

Janet's Story

When Janet found out she was HIV-positive, the counselor at the testing site told her that she needed to see a doctor as soon as possible to begin treatment. Janet was sixteen years old, had no job, and had no money saved up. She knew she would have to tell her parents about her illness in order to take care of herself.

Janet and her friend, Halle, wrote down what Janet wanted to say to her parents, and Janet spent several days memorizing it until she felt she was ready.

After dinner one night, Janet asked her parents to come into the living room.

"I have something very important to tell you," Janet said as her parents sat down on the couch. "I need you to let me finish before you ask me any questions. OK?"

Her parents nodded.

Janet looked over the notes that she and Halle had written out, and then she began. "First, I want to tell you that I love you very much. I would do anything not to have to tell you this, but I don't have any choice." She took a deep breath before she went on. "I tested positive for HIV two weeks ago." Then, more quickly, she said, "I'm scared to death, and I just want you to love me and help me."

Although there is no way to tell your parents that can guarantee they will react the way you want them to, Janet chose a way that she hoped would minimize an angry reaction. She was not defensive. She did not blame anyone. She used "I" sentences, telling her parents how she felt. Although Janet did not say she was sorry, she did let her parents know that she wished the situation were different. Finally, she let her parents know what she wanted from them: love and help.

If, no matter how hard you try, you just can't tell your parents that you are HIV-positive, you may have to get someone to tell them for you. If you have a relative you can confide in, that could be okay. Maybe you know an HIV counselor who would be willing to help you tell your parents. If having someone else tell your parents is not a choice you like, you can write them a letter saying the things that Janet said to her parents.

Your Parents' Reaction

Your parents may react to the news that you are HIV-positive in many of the same ways that you did when you first learned your diagnosis. They may be shocked and unable to respond. They may be fearful, afraid of what others will think. Or they may be angry—angry at you or at themselves or angry at the person they feel is responsible. They may feel guilty and blame themselves, or they may blame you. You should be prepared for any or all of these reactions. Although there is no way to predict how someone will react, if you have thought about possible reactions beforehand, it may be easier for you to respond.

DEALING WITH FEARFUL PARENTS

Fear is a very common response to HIV. Fear can occur because your parents have little information about HIV. They may be afraid that you will die soon. They may be afraid that you are contagious. They may be afraid that they won't be able to care for you. One of the best ways to fight fear is with information. You know that HIV is not spread by casual contact, but maybe your parents don't. Help them get the information they need to understand exactly what HIV is and what it does. Remind your parents that you are not sick now and that today is what is important. If your parents are afraid of what might happen to you, it may be that you are the one who has to reassure them. That may be hard, especially at a time when you are wanting them to reassure you. As your parents become more informed and less afraid about HIV, they will be able to help you more.

Some parents may be most afraid of what the neighbors will do and think. There have been many stories about the discrimination experienced by HIV-positive people. Remind your parents that there are laws against discrimination. You cannot be asked to leave your home, your neighborhood, your school, or your job just because you are HIV-positive. The same rights apply to those who care for someone who is HIV-positive. Read Chapter 8, "Your Responsibilities and Rights."

If your parents continue to seem concerned about what the neighbors will think, it can feel very hurtful. *You* know that the neighbors don't have to be told, but maybe your parents don't. Give your parents the facts. If they remain fearful, ask them to speak to an HIV counselor. Tell your parents that you feel hurt when they seem more concerned about the neighbors than about you. You have a right to let your parents know how you feel.

DEALING WITH ANGRY PARENTS

Seventeen-year-old Adrianna told her mother, Connie, that she had contracted HIV from having unprotected sex with her boyfriend, Luis. She was sure her mother was going to be very angry with her. Instead, her mother became very angry at Luis. Although Luis, an intravenous drug user, had contracted the disease from using dirty needles, Connie accused him of having sex with other girls in the neighborhood. She refused to allow him to visit her daughter or even talk to her on the phone. Connie called Luis's mother and told her that her son had HIV and was spreading the disease around the neighborhood. She also called all the people who knew Luis and told them that he had given her daughter AIDS and that they should keep their daughters away from him. Before long Luis had lost his job, and Adrianna had been asked to leave school. People were afraid of being exposed to the virus and began sending hate mail to both Adrianna and Luis. Connie had to call the police more than once to complain about anonymous phone calls.

Connie had created more problems than there needed to be. She took an important sense of control from Adrianna and caused unnecessary problems. It is easy to understand why Connie was angry at Luis, but her anger did absolutely nothing to help her daughter.

If your parent reacts as Connie did, the best thing you can do is stay out of the way. Connie created hysteria in the neighborhood because she misdirected her anger and because she, as well as many of the neighbors, knew very little about HIV and AIDS. The result was discrimination and fear.

It is against the law to be forced out of school or a job because of testing HIV-positive. Unfortunately, both things occur. Although Luis could have been fired because he used illegal drugs, in fact he was fired because Connie's mother had convinced his employer that he had AIDS. Sometimes, there is no way to repair the damage done in a case like Adrianna's. If you think your parent may overreact as Connie did, you might consider having an HIV counselor help you tell your parent about your diagnosis. The counselor could emphasize the problems that could develop if your parent acts without thinking.

What do you do if your parents respond with anger toward you? It is not uncommon to react to bad news with anger. Usually, as the person becomes used to the news, the anger fades. If your parent's initial reaction is anger at you, try not to respond with anger. It may be difficult, especially if you think your parent is being unfair.

Danny's Story

Danny was an occasional drug user who contracted the virus by sharing needles with friends. Two months before his high school graduation, he found out he was HIV-positive. He had lived alone with his mother since she and his father had divorced. The night before the graduation ceremony, he decided that he had to tell his mother about his diagnosis. She became infuriated.

"My God! What will the neighbors say?" she shouted. "We'll be kicked out of our apartment. I'll lose my job. And all because of you!" She continued screaming at Danny until he left the house.

The next day Danny returned home to get ready for graduation, but his mother refused to let him in. She had piled all his clothes in the hallway outside their apartment. She said he had ruined her life and she never wanted to see him again. Danny left, wondering what to do next.

Not all families are caring, loving families. In many households, members physically and emotionally abuse one another. Some families' strength has been diminished by the alcoholism or substance abuse of one or more of the members. In some families people simply don't know how to care for one another. Such families are called dysfunctional families.

It may be hard to tell your parents that you have HIV if you live in a dysfunctional family, but you still must try.

A parent may become so angry and out of control that you are forced to leave home. If that happens and you have no other place to go, you need to find a children's shelter. Although you may not consider yourself a child, the law considers you one if you are not legally emancipated. In most states a person becomes legally emancipated at the age of eighteen. That means that you can sign contracts, seek medical attention on your own, and live away from home. In short, you are legally responsible for your own care and your own actions. In some states a person who has joined the military or who is married is considered emancipated even if they are under the age of eighteen. Outside of those possibilities, you are still considered a child. By going to a shelter or a crisis center, you can find someone who can help you decide what to do next.

If there is no shelter or crisis center in your area, contact a teacher or a religious leader to get advice. It may be that you need to be legally emancipated from your parents. You may go to live in a foster home. Or your parent may calm down and you can return home. Each person's circumstances are different.

DEALING WITH A BLAMING PARENT

Blame can take two routes. Your parents may blame themselves or even each other, or they may blame you.

Ira's Story

When Ira first told his parents that he was HIV-positive, he didn't tell them that he had contracted the virus while having unprotected homosexual sex. Although Ira had been aware of his sexual orientation for four years, he had worked very hard to keep his parents from knowing. He knew that sooner or later his parents would ask how he had become infected, and he decided to tell them the truth. His parents took the news very quietly, but later Ira heard them arguing in the bedroom. His father was shouting at his mother that it was her fault, that she treated Ira like a mama's boy. His mother was crying. The next day, neither of his parents would look at him or each other.

What could Ira have done when his parents wouldn't look at him? He could have asked them how they felt about what he had told them. He couldn't tell whether they were ashamed of him or themselves. Sometimes it is hard for parents to hear that a child is homosexual; they often don't know how to react. Ira's concern was not about his sexuality, but about the fact that he had HIV. His parents were too busy blaming themselves and each other to notice that Ira needed them.

Telling your parents that you are gay can often distract them from the real issue of you being HIV-positive. It may be up to you to remind them of their real concerns. You may suggest that they go to a counselor with you. You can also get information for them from any gay crisis center. Your parents may not understand homosexuality. They may not be aware that a person is born with his or her sexual orientation already in place. The more information you can give them, the easier it will be for them to reex-amine their reactions and to learn to help you cope with being HIV-positive.

While Ira's parents blamed themselves and each other for the crisis, it is possible your parents may blame you. When this happens, the blame is often disguised by sus-picious accusations.

Linda's Story

Linda's parents were very supportive when she told them she was HIV-positive. They immediately made arrangements for her to receive medical care and professional counseling. Linda had told her parents that she believed she had contracted HIV by having unprotected sex with an intravenous drug user. She also said that she had stopped seeing this person. For a few months everything seemed to be going fine at home.

One night, Linda planned to spend the night at a girlfriend's house. It was to be her first time out since her diagnosis. Her parents had a fit. They accused her of planning to meet her old boyfriend and said she could not go out. Hoping that they would calm down if she stayed home, Linda canceled her plans. But the next week, when she wanted to go bowling with a friend, her parents had the same reaction. Although Linda had always been honest with her parents, she began sneaking out of the house after they'd gone to sleep.

It is not uncommon for parents to imagine all sorts of things after a crisis. Although Linda's parents worried that she was going to meet her old boyfriend, they could just as easily have accused her of going out to use drugs. If your parent constantly accuses you of engaging in a dangerous behavior that you are *not* involved in, try to have an open discussion with him or her. You might suggest that your parent go with you to a counseling session where you could try to work the situation out with a safe third party.

It may seem that a lot of what you can or need to do revolves around a professional counselor. That is because it is not easy to cope with HIV alone. HIV counselors are experienced in dealing with a variety of reactions from parents and teenagers. They know what resources are available to help you and your family. A professional counselor can help guide you and your family as you work through your problems together. Being HIV-positive is hard enough without trying to do everything by yourself.

CHAPTER 7

Telling Your Friends

T elling someone you are HIV-positive can be very difficult, especially if you are uncertain about how that person will react.

Remember that you don't have to tell everyone. The only people you must tell are those whom you may have exposed to the virus, your health-care provider, and your dentist.

It is your decision to tell anyone else. But you need to think very carefully before you decide. Ask yourself why you want to tell the person. Do you care for him or her? Does he or she care for you? Do you think telling will make you feel better? Can you trust the person not to tell others? Do you value the person's advice and friendship? If you answered yes to all these questions, you probably will decide to tell the person. If, however, you answered no to any of the questions, think again before you speak.

Once you have decided to tell someone, the problem is actually doing it. If you are receiving counseling or are in an HIV support group, ask your counselor or members of your support group for tips on what to say. Their experiences may help make telling easier for you. But there is no set way to tell anyone. It is different for each person.

Hector and Joshua

Joshua was surprised when Hector called and asked him to come over. He hadn't seen Hector in over two months. Hector had been acting very strange and depressed. Whenever Josh had asked him what was wrong, Hector yelled at him to mind his own business. Finally Josh had become tired of Hector's anger and insults, so he had stayed away. It was hard because the boys had been friends for twelve years, since they were three years old.

Josh could tell that something was wrong by the sound of Hector's voice on the phone. He decided not to say anything about Hector's bad moods until he knew what was going on.

Joshua went to Hector's and found him sitting on the floor in a corner of the room he shared with his younger brother. Joshua thought he looked awful but was afraid to say anything. The two boys just looked at each other for a few minutes. Finally Joshua broke the silence.

"Hi, Hector. How's it goin', man?"

Then Hector started to cry. Joshua just stood there for a moment. Then he put his arms around Hector and held him while Hector continued to cry. Finally Hector calmed down a bit and told Josh that he had found out he was HIV-positive. Josh resisted an impulse to let go of his friend. He knew enough about HIV to be aware that you could not "catch" it from embracing someone, so he continued to hug Hector.

"I'm sorry, man," Josh said. "I'm sorry."

After some time, Hector finally began to talk. He told Joshua how a girl that he had had unprotected sex with a few times had called him and told him that she was infected and that he should get tested in case she had passed the virus on to him.

"I wanted to tell you before. I've known for a while. I just didn't know what you'd say."

One reason it is hard for someone who is HIV-positive to tell a friend is because he or she may be afraid of the reaction. If Joshua had pulled away, how do you think Hector would have felt? How would you feel if you told someone you were HIV-positive and that person pulled away from you? A friend's initial reaction to hearing that you are HIV-positive may indeed be to pull away. That does not mean the person is not your friend. Your friend may have reacted without thinking or may not know that HIV is not spread by casual contact. Don't judge a friend by first reactions.

Did you notice that Joshua did not ask his friend how he became infected? It is often just as hard for someone who is HIV-positive to reveal how he or she contracted the virus as it is to tell someone that he or she is infected. Sometimes it is even harder.

Tony and Julius

Like Hector and Joshua, Tony and Julius had been friends for most of their lives. When Tony found out he had contracted HIV from having unprotected sex, he was really frightened. Not only did he face telling his family and friends that he was HIV-positive, he was also faced with revealing that he was gay and that he had most likely become infected through homosexual intercourse. Tony had never told Julius that he was gay for fear of losing his friendship. Julius was always talking about girls and making jokes about gay people. Nevertheless, Tony enjoyed being with Julius even if it meant hiding his sexual orientation. Tony had never told his family that he was gay, either. One day Tony decided he didn't want to keep so many secrets anymore. He wanted to find a way to tell Julius that he was gay and that he had tested positive for HIV. Because he was scared, he decided to act as if he were talking about someone else.

"Hey, Jules, did I tell you about my cousin Marino? The family thinks he's got HIV."

"Wow, no kidding? I always thought he was kinda funny, you know?" Julius answered, wiggling his hips.

At that point, Tony decided against telling Julius, so he said, "Well, some of the family thinks it, not everyone. Besides, he's going with Gina, so he's not 'funny'."

Tony had no way of knowing how Julius would react. But he obviously made the right decision not to tell his friend. And Julius, by being judgmental and making fun of another person's sexual orientation, lost a chance to be a true friend.

Sometimes friends give us information in a roundabout way. If you have a friend who starts talking about HIV, be open to the possibility that he or she may be trying to confide in you. Saying things out of ignorance, the way Julius did, could cost you a friendship that you value.

If you are uncertain or afraid of someone's reaction, first try talking to that person about your problem as if it affected someone else. You can use words like "if" and "maybe." Try to get your friend to talk about HIV and AIDS. That way, you may be able to correct any misinformation before you tell. It may be that your friend will react differently to a hypothetical situation than a real one. Only you can decide if you really want to tell.

But if your friend makes jokes about AIDS or gay people the way Julius did, you need to be careful. Having HIV is not a joke, no matter who it is or how that person was infected.

Suppose you tell someone you believe is your friend, and he or she turns away from you. That's what happened to Jon when he told his friend Bruce that he was gay and HIV-positive.

Jon's Story

Jon learned he was HIV-positive when he tried to donate blood during a fraternity blood drive. He had never worried about getting infected, but he wasn't really surprised. He had been having unprotected gay sex for six years. Although many people he knew at college were aware that he was gay, he had kept his sexual orientation a secret from his friends at home.

When Jon went home for Thanksgiving break, he decided it was time to tell Bruce, his best friend from high school, that he was gay and HIV-positive. Bruce picked Jon up at the airport as he always did. On the drive home, Jon told Bruce he was HIV-positive. Bruce didn't say anything, so Jon kept talking. He said that he was gay and that he had contracted the virus from having unprotected sex. Bruce still said nothing, just kept driving. When they got to Jon's house, Bruce just sat in the car. Jon realized that he was having a problem with what he had heard, but Jon thought it would pass. He carried his bags into the house. When he went back out to say goodbye to Bruce, his friend had already driven off.

The next day Jon called Bruce's house, but there was no answer. He left a message on the answering machine. Bruce didn't call back. Jon thought for sure that Bruce would visit on Thanksgiving, but he didn't. Finally, the day before he was to go back to school, Jon walked over to Bruce's house to try and talk to his friend. Bruce's mother answered the door. She said that Bruce was not at home and that she would appreciate it if Jon never came to their house again. Jon knew that he had lost a friend.

Unfortunately, Jon and Bruce's case is not uncommon. You need to prepare yourself for rejection from people you thought were your friends. It won't be easy, and it may hurt you very much. The thing to remember is that many people are uninformed about sexual orientation and HIV, and people tend to fear what they do not understand. Bruce and his mother were not afraid of Jon. They were afraid of his sexual orientation and of HIV. Try to remember that any rejection you experience has more to do with fear of the disease than it does with you.

Sometimes you can help your friend understand the truth about sexual orientation and HIV before you tell him or her that you are infected. Try talking about HIV in general terms, about what it is and what it isn't, about how you can get it and how you can't. Do the same thing about homosexuality. Talk about sexual orientation in general terms. If you can educate a friend before you tell him or her, you may avoid rejection.

If your friend continues to reject you, prepare to let that friendship go. You cannot force people to listen or to learn.

If you are having trouble dealing with your feelings toward someone who turned away from you because you are HIV-positive, you may need to talk to a counselor. If you belong to a support group, discuss your feelings with the other members. Some of them may be able to offer suggestions that will help you deal with rejection and move on with your life. Don't let the ignorance of a few people affect other parts of your life.

It may seem unfair that all the burden of understanding is on you. After all, you are the one who has HIV. Because you are the one who will be hurt by rejection or careless comments, you are the one who must decide if you want to tell someone. Because you are the one who is educated about sexual orientation and HIV, it is up to you to help educate those around you. If you feel this is too much for you to do, you need to think very carefully before you tell anyone that you have HIV or are gay. You should talk to a counselor or someone you trust before telling other people.

CHAPTER 8

Your Responsibilities and Rights

Because many people with HIV experience discrimination, it is important to know what your rights are and what they are not. It is just as important to know what your responsibilities are.

Your legal responsibilities vary from state to state. Some states have passed laws that obligate you to tell anyone you may have exposed to the virus. You are further obligated to tell any present or future sex partners or people with whom you share drug paraphernalia that you have the virus. If you refuse to reveal this information as required, your health-care provider may be required by law to do it for you. Sometimes public health departments or health-care providers inform persons you may have exposed to the virus without revealing your name. But no matter how these people are informed, it is your legal obligation to inform them that they may be at risk. If you fail to meet your legal obligation, your family may be sued. Even if no legal action is taken, you will still want to examine your conscience. You have a moral obligation to tell those you have put at risk. This moral obligation is more important than the legal obligation.

You are obligated to tell your doctor and your dentist about your diagnosis. If informed, your doctor and dentist can take precautions to avoid accidentally exposing themselves to the virus.

If you work in a health-care agency, such as a hospital or nursing home, you are probably obligated to tell your employer. You are under no obligation to tell anyone else.

You cannot give blood or be an organ donor. If you are pregnant when you learn you are HIV-positive, you need to consider the risks to yourself and the fetus.

YOUR RIGHTS

Your rights are a little more complex because the law surrounding HIV and AIDS is still evolving. Many issues connected with these illnesses have not yet been addressed, and new laws are constantly being introduced. The following information will help you understand some of your rights. You may have other rights, depending on where you live.

CONFIDENTIALITY ISSUES

Your right not to have your HIV status disclosed is limited. Generally, your medical records are confidential, and physicians must protect that confidentiality within certain boundaries. Doctors in all fifty states must report every AIDS case they treat to the state public health department. Twenty-seven states require reporting of all HIV-positive tests. This reporting is done usually by name or social security number. The state health department may not reveal your name, although it is required to report the number of AIDS cases within its jurisdiction to the federal government. The new home tests for HIV ensure you total confidentiality because your test is identified by a three–digit code.

Your right to confidentiality may also be dependent upon your meeting your responsibility to others. You must inform everyone you put at risk for infection. If you knowingly fail to do so, you may be sued. If you refuse to tell those whom you may have exposed to the virus, your physician has at least a moral obligation to inform them. In some states, your physician may be legally obliged to reveal your diagnosis and your name if you refuse to notify people you may have put at risk. Your HIV status may also be revealed to anyone who has a right to your complete medical records. However, those who rightfully have access to your medical records and, therefore, your HIV status are under legal obligation to maintain your confidentially unless the law requires them to do otherwise. In some states, your medical records may be requested by your employer *with your consent*. You cannot be required to grant that consent. You are under no legal obligation to report your HIV status to your family members, friends, neighbors, or employers.

All these laws and rules about confidentiality are good, but they are of little help to you when it comes to treatment. Unless you are emancipated from your parents and have your own source of income, you probably will have to tell your parents or guardians about your diagnosis in order to get financial help for medical treatment.

Although some states allow minors to consent to treatment, that does not mean that the treatment is free. Usually if you cannot pay for the service at the time, a bill will be sent to you or your parents at home. Would your parents pay a medical bill if they had no idea what it was for? Probably not. So you see, there is a dilemma when it comes to paying for treatment and not telling your parents or guardians.

DISCRIMINATION ISSUES

It is against the law to discriminate against someone because he or she is HIV-positive. Nevertheless, discrimination is a fact of life for many infected people and their families. Some laws can protect you, but only if you are aware of their existence. Following are some of the major laws pertaining to people infected with HIV. There may be others applicable to your area.

Federal Laws

The Rehabilitation Act of 1973, Section 504, protects all citizens regardless of race, creed, sex, color, or handicap against discrimination by any organization or service provider who receives money from federal funds, either directly or indirectly. AIDS is included in the handicapped definition. This law was strengthened in 1990 by the Americans with Disabilities Act. It is now against the law to discriminate against someone with HIV even if the service provider or organization receives no money from the federal government. This means that you cannot be fired from a job simply because you are HIV-positive. It means that you have the right to the same medical services as someone who is not HIV-positive. It means that you are entitled to receive any social services for which you are eligible, regardless of your HIV status.

To get more information about your civil rights under federal law, call the U.S. Department of Health and Human Services, Office for Civil Rights, Philadelphia, (215) 596-6109. Ask for the Equal Opportunity Specialist.

To file a complaint when you believe you have been discriminated against, write:

Office for Civil Rights
U.S. Department of Health and Human Services
P.O. Box 13716
Philadelphia, PA 19101

Your complaint must be filed within six months after the incident. In your letter of complaint, be sure to include your name and phone number, the names of your parents or guardians if they are still legally responsible for you, and the organization or service provider about which you are complaining. Be sure to say that HIV is the basis of your handicap. Describe what happened and when it happened (remember the six-month deadline). State what, if anything, you or the service provider did to try to resolve the situation.

Even if a situation was resolved, you may want to file a complaint to put the service provider on notice that discrimination is against the law.

State Laws

Most states have laws that forbid discrimination based upon a handicap or disability. In many states, HIV is considered a handicap or disability. If this is so in your state, you are probably protected under state law against discrimination in accommodations. Depending upon the state, public accommodations may include restaurants, hospitals, schools, beauty shops, and doctors' offices. To learn what is covered, call your state human relations commission or civil rights commission.

EDUCATION ISSUES

The Rehabilitation Act of 1973 (PL93-112), Section 504, provides: "No otherwise qualified handicapped individual in the United States . . . shall, solely by reason of his handicap, be excluded from participation in, be denied the benefits of, or be subjected to discrimination under any program or activity receiving federal financial assistance."

The Department of Justice includes asymptomatic HIV infection and AIDS under Section 504. If you are not in need of special education but are moved to a special education class after a diagnosis of HIV and solely because of a diagnosis of HIV, that move is illegal. Your parents or guardians have a right to demand that you be returned to the regular classroom. The National Association of State Boards of Education has notified its members that removing children to special education classes strictly because of their HIV status could allow the school system to be sued. If you are HIV-positive, however, you should avoid being in classrooms with people who have infectious diseases like chicken pox because you are more vulnerable to infection.

Neither you nor your parents or guardians are under legal or moral obligation to notify your teachers or school administrators of your HIV status.

In 1987, in the case *School Board of Nassau County v. Arline*, the U.S. Supreme Court reaffirmed the protection of Section 504 for those with contagious diseases. HIV is considered a contagious disease in many states. In addition, discrimination is forbidden under the 1990 Americans with Disabilities Act (ADA); this includes those who are infected with HIV.

MEDICAL TREATMENT

You cannot be turned away from a hospital because of your HIV status. That, however, does not guarantee that you will be treated at any particular hospital. Some hospitals may not have the kinds of services you may need; they are under no obligation to treat you, but they are under obligation to direct you to a hospital that does provide those services. Some doctors may refuse to treat someone who is HIV-positive because they do not consider themselves sufficiently skilled in the treatment of HIV patients. If you had a doctor before you were diagnosed as HIV-positive, he or she is obligated either to treat you or find someone who will treat you. It is illegal for a doctor to "abandon" an established patient. You and your parent or guardian have a right to be treated with respect and dignity whether or not the doctor or hospital feels capable of treating you.

Dentists are under the same obligations as doctors. A dentist may decide not to treat you because he or she does not feel able to provide proper care. A dentist you saw before your diagnosis is under obligation to refer you to someone who will treat you if he or she cannot.

Even if you are aware of all of your rights, discrimination may occur. Although there are private legal means that you and your parents or guardians can pursue to guarantee your rights, it is often an expensive and time-consuming process. Sometimes it is enough to contact the civil rights or human resources agency in your area. They will contact the person or agency with whom you were dealing, and generally the discriminatory behavior can be stopped. But it is up to you to decide which battles are important enough to fight. If you decide to change doctors or to find a new dentist or a new barber because you think your current ones would turn you away, that's okay. Ask your HIV counselor or members of your support group or call an AIDS crisis center for the names of members of the community who understand the myths and facts about HIV. It might be easier for you to see people you know are sympathetic to those with HIV. No matter what you decide, the decision you make is the one that's right for you.

CHAPTER 9

Your Health Needs

Being HIV-positive does not mean that you have lost control over your health and your body. In fact, being HIV-positive means more than ever that you must take proper care of your body. Many things can happen that you cannot prevent, but there are also many things that you can control. Diet, exercise, and stress-reducing activities are all important aspects of life for someone with HIV.

TAKING CARE OF YOUR BODY

Nutrition

Nutrition is always important, but it becomes even more important to a person who is HIV-positive. Good nutrition helps to maintain the immune system. Also, people with HIV tend to lose weight, and it is important to do whatever you can to postpone weight loss. Following a nutritious diet can help.

Meat should make up about 25 percent of your diet for the following reasons:

- HIV depletes vitamin B_{12}, so a diet rich in vitamin B_{12} is recommended. Red meat is the best source.
- HIV depletes cholesterol, so foods high in cholesterol and nutrition are needed. Lamb is a good meat source for high cholesterol and nutrition.

If you are a vegetarian or avoid meat for other reasons, you probably should get vitamin B_{12} supplements. These are available as injections or as intranasal supplementation. Ask your health-care provider about supplemental vitamins. Also ask about food lists and cookbooks. Your doctor may have this information in the office or will be able to tell you where you can get it. Or call the HIV and AIDS hot line and ask for the names of cookbooks or simply some recipes that would provide nutritious, good-tasting foods.

Drink at least two quarts of water a day. If your T4-cell count is less than 100, you should drink only water that has been distilled or carbon-block filtered. Water is important to prevent dehydration. The skin is less resilient when it is dry; that makes it more liable to crack and more prone to little cuts, both of which can let infection in. By drinking enough water and using a moisturizer, you can help your skin maintain its resiliency and remain effective as your primary guard against infection.

If you are losing weight, you need to eat high-calorie foods that are nutritious. High-calorie drink supplements such as Ensure, Enrich, and others are available in grocery stores and drugstores.

Try to avoid the following:

- Sugars and sweeteners. Some sweeteners contain carcinogens. Also, it is possible that some of these products make it easier for viruses to grow. Sugar is especially bad for people with the mouth infection thrush because it helps the fungus to grow. If you do not have thrush and are experiencing weight loss, go ahead and use sugar.

- White flour. As a processed food, it is much harder to digest than products made from whole grain flour.
- Pork. Pork is hard to digest. Although cooking kills the bacteria in pork, the bacteria still remain in the food. If you do have pork, be certain that it is completely cooked.
- Raw fruits and vegetables. Always wash these to remove any chemical residues and bacteria on the raw skin. Then peel fruits and steam vegetables to remove any remaining bacteria.
- **Never** eat raw fish, raw eggs, or rare red meat.

Vitamin/Mineral Therapy

Some people believe that taking a lot of vitamins will speed their recovery from illness. Be careful. Taking a normal daily vitamin supplement is probably okay; ask your doctor. Do not treat yourself with megadoses of vitamins or minerals without consulting your doctor. Excessive doses of certain vitamins and minerals can be dangerous.

- Vitamin A. Some people believe that large doses of this vitamin will increase the growth of CD4 cells. The Recommended Daily Amount (RDA) of vitamin A is 3,000 International Units (IU). Studies have shown that excessive amounts (100,000 or more IUs per day for three months) can cause liver damage, vomiting, headaches, hair loss, sore mouth, and dry itchy skin.

- Vitamin C. Although large amounts of vitamin C are said to fight colds and cancer, this has not been proven. The RDA of vitamin C is 60 milligrams. Excessive amounts can corrode the teeth and cause stomach pain and diarrhea.
- Selenium. The body seems to contain less selenium during the later stages of HIV than in the earlier stages. Taking excessive amounts of selenium can damage cells and make your situation worse.
- Zinc. Like selenium, zinc appears to be depleted in the bodies of people during the later stages of HIV. Excessive amounts of zinc can cause nausea and vomiting. Before you take more than the RDA of any vitamin or mineral, consult your doctor.

Treating Infections

People who are HIV-positive are more susceptible to a variety of infections because their immune system is not fully functional. Many of these infections are easily treatable, especially if they are treated early. By knowing these infections and the simple ways to prevent or treat them, you can take control of your health care and make life a little easier. The following are just some of the infections that people who are HIV-positive are prone to. You may experience all of them, some of them, or none of them. By talking with your health-care provider about what to expect, you will be better able to take care of yourself.

Caring for Your Mouth

Good dental health is especially important to someone who is HIV-positive, for several reasons. Mouth, gum, and tooth pain can inhibit the appetite. Maintaining a nutritious diet is extremely important if you are HIV-positive, but if it hurts every time you eat, you are less likely to eat as much or as well as you should.

People with HIV are more prone to gingivitis and periodontitis. Gingivitis is an inflammation of the gums, which usually causes bleeding. If the gingivitis is severe, the result can be periodontitis, which is the loss of gum and bone tissue and ultimately loss of teeth. The usual way to treat gingivitis and periodontitis is by using germ-killing mouthwashes such as Listerine or Betadine, which do not require a prescription, or Peridex, which does. Brush several times a day with a soft toothbrush, and make flossing part of your daily mouth care. See your dentist regularly, probably more often than you did before you learned you had HIV.

Mouth Infections

Having HIV makes it more likely that you will contract a variety of mouth infections such as thrush, oral hairy leukoplakia, herpes simplex, or aphthous ulcers. These infections are not prevented by brushing and flossing, but practicing good oral hygiene may help you notice the infections so that they can be treated early.

- Thrush is caused by the fungus *Candida albicans*. It is a common mouth fungus, but when it gets out of control it can be painful. Most people with HIV

develop thrush when taking antibiotics. Antibiotics inhibit bacteria growth, both good and bad.
By hindering the growth of good bacteria in the
mouth, they also make it easier for thrush to
occur.

The symptoms of thrush are white or grayish
patches on your gums or tongue or on the inside of
your cheeks. You may feel nothing, or you may have
severe pain that makes it difficult to chew or
swallow.

Thrush usually clears up in one or two weeks by
treatment with prescription drugs such as nystatin,
clotrimazole (Lotrimin), ketoconazole (Nizoral), or
fluconazole (Diflucan).

- Oral hairy leukoplakia seems to affect only people
  with HIV, and it is not contagious. The symptoms
  are white patches containing very tiny hairs on the
  tongue. The mouth is usually sore, but it may not
  be. A common treatment is acyclovir (Zovirax),
  which is an antiviral drug. The patches usually dis-
  appear in a few weeks.

- Herpes simplex. You probably already know this as
  fever blisters or cold sores. It is not a dangerous
  condition, but it *is* contagious. Be careful about
  kissing or sharing drinking containers or straws.
  The symptoms are raised watery blisters on the lips
  or in the mouth. The blisters can be painful, and if
  in the mouth they can make it hard to chew or
  swallow. A variety of over-the-counter treatments
  may be helpful, such as Blistex, Anbusol, and
  others. Acyclovir (Zovirax) is also used in treatment
  of herpes simplex.

- Aphthous ulcers. The cause of aphthous ulcers is
  unknown, but people with and without HIV have

them. They are not contagious, but they can be painful and affect your appetite.

Aphthous ulcers, sometimes called "canker sores," may look a little like herpes simplex, but they are not the same. They occur inside the mouth, usually on the cheeks, but also on the gums or the tongue. Nonprescription remedies are easy to find. Rinsing your mouth with Lidocaine and taking Benadryl orally is usually effective. If the ulcers persist or are very severe, your doctor may prescribe corticosteroids.

Some other precautions you can take in mouth care: Use a clean towel every day. Do not use anyone else's towel. Do not use anyone else's toothbrush. Clean your own toothbrush in peroxide and water for fifteen minutes once a week. Remember, you are vulnerable to infection from other people if you are HIV-positive.

Caring for Your Skin

As you know, your skin is your first line of defense against disease, so it is very important to take care of it. Certain skin problems that are common to many people can be more severe in someone who is HIV-positive.

- *Molluscum contagiosum* is a virus that is mainly considered a cosmetic nuisance. It causes small, skin-colored, indented bumps, usually around the mouth or genitals. Antibiotics have no effect on this virus, but the bumps are easily removed by a dermatologist.
- Seborrhea on the scalp is called dandruff. It also appears on the face, ears, chest, and genitals in red, scaly patches.

You can treat dandruff by using an over-the-counter dandruff shampoo. For patches elsewhere, nonprescription cortisone ointments generally do the trick. Consult your health-care provider before treating yourself.

• Shingles, also known as herpes zoster, is contagious for people who have never had chicken pox, including adults. If you develop this condition, be careful to prevent transmission to others. Shingles causes blisters that look like chicken pox. The blisters travel in bands along the nerve paths and may affect only one section of the body. It can be very painful, but it is not life-threatening. If it does not clear up by itself, acyclovir (Zovirax) is usually prescribed.

• Athlete's foot and ringworm are skin infections caused by a fungus. Athlete's foot is patches of red, flaking skin on the feet. When it is around the groin area, it is called jock itch. Ringworm is circular patches of red, flaky skin on the scalp or skin. A variety of over-the-counter products are used to combat these infections. Ringworm can be treated with clotrimazole (Lotrimin). Fingernails and toenails may become infected by a fungus, becoming thick and discolored. Your health-care provider can prescribe antibiotics to help control this.

• Allergic rashes. If you are on any medication and you develop a rash on your chest, back, arms, legs, or face, you may be having an allergic reaction to medication. You may also have a fever, difficulty breathing, itching, and welts. Call your health-care provider immediately. You will probably be taken off the medication and be given an antihistamine to treat the rash.

Remember, being HIV-positive means that your body may not be able to fight back as strongly as it needs to under certain circumstances. If you feel you have a problem, don't delay. Call someone.

Exercise

Exercise is very important for the person who is HIV-positive, not only because it helps maintain body strength but also because it makes you feel better. There may be days when you are simply too tired to do any exercise at all. That's okay, but try to get in at least a little exercise when you are feeling stronger. Ask a friend to take a walk or go bike riding. Get outside as much as you can. It not only gives you physical exercise but can provide much-needed mental exercise too. Try to get in some "workout" time. Aerobic exercise is known to release endorphins, which are the body's natural painkillers. The release of endorphins also helps your emotional well-being. And, as you know, the emotions affect the immune system. You don't have to wear yourself out, but find some kind of exercise that you enjoy and can do regularly.

Meditation and Relaxation Therapy

Just as it is important to take care of your body through nutrition, medical care, and exercise, it is essential to take care of the emotional side of your life. It cannot be overstated that stress helps to weaken the immune system. In today's world, everyone is subject to stress; having HIV only increases the load. Meditation and relaxation therapy are commonly prescribed for people with illnesses like HIV. Many books, tapes, and videos are on the market to help you meditate and relax. Your doctor or your support group may be able to recommend some.

The principles of meditation and relaxation therapy are simple. You find a quiet place to sit or lie down. You slowly relax your body from your toes to your head as you take slow, deep breaths in and out. You may imagine going to a beautiful place, a sanctuary that you design in your mind. You may imagine meeting a wise person who can give you the understanding you need. Or you may just listen to the simple sounds around you. You might try putting on some soft music while you take a warm bath. Whatever is right for you, be sure to take time out and do it.

Remember, stress affects the immune system, so take a deep breath before you get anxious about something. Think: Is this something I can do anything about? If it is, start to take care of it. If it isn't, try to let it go.

CHAPTER 10

Treating HIV

YOU AND YOUR DOCTOR

How often have you gone to a doctor and not understood a word that he or she said to you? If you answered "Almost all the time," you are not alone. Sometimes doctors forget that not everyone has gone to medical school. Because it is important for you to understand what is happening to your body, you need to understand what your doctor is saying. If your doctor describes a procedure or treatment that doesn't make any sense to you, ask for clarification. You have a right to have it explained in words that you understand. You are a consumer, and your doctor is providing a service. If your doctor is impatient or tells you that you don't need to know, say, "I would feel more comfortable if you would explain." If you can't bring yourself to do that, take a parent with you and have him or her ask the questions. Ask for pamphlets or booklets on the procedures or medications your doctor is suggesting. If you still are not clear about what is going on, call your health clinic or AIDS center. Don't go on without having all the information you want.

Another difficult topic to discuss with doctors is the cost of treatment and medication. Because doctor's fees and the prices of medicines are not regulated by law, it is extremely important to get these figures. They can vary from state to state, city to city, hospital to hospital, and doctor to doctor. If your doctor states that he or she doesn't handle the bookkeeping and so cannot tell you the cost of your treatment and medication, ask to speak with the person who does know the potential costs. You have a right to know what you will be expected to pay. Also, ask about all available payment options. Treating HIV can be very expensive, and you will probably have to devise a payment schedule with your health-care provider.

Your time is as valuable as anyone else's. It is becoming more and more common for doctors to schedule several appointments at the same time. If your health-care provider keeps you waiting long after the scheduled appointment time, you have a right to ask why. Keep in mind that your doctor's priority is to treat emergencies, which may be causing the delay. However, if your doctor is continually late in seeing you, you have every right to look for another doctor. If you are getting angry every time you see your doctor, you are not doing much good for yourself. Ask at AIDS crisis centers or support groups for medical recommendations.

You may also be nervous about discussing your illness with your doctor. When you are nervous, you can forget to ask things you want to know and forget things you are told. Take paper and a pencil with you when you visit your doctor. Write down what is said or ask your doctor to write it down. List any questions you want to ask at your next visit, and check them off one by one as they are answered.

Remember, you are the consumer. Your doctor is there to serve you. Being a patient does not take away any of your rights or diminish your intelligence. The better informed you are the easier it is to cope.

TREATMENTS AND MEDICATIONS

Doctors approach HIV treatment on three levels. They try to inhibit the growth of the virus, they try to guard against and treat opportunistic infections such as pneumonia and tuberculosis, and they treat the symptoms of noninfectious problems such as nausea, insomnia, anxiety, and depression. New treatments and medications are being used at each level of the approach. When your doctor speaks with you about treatment, be sure to ask if it reflects the most recent medical research.

Treatment of HIV has changed dramatically in the past few years and will continue to change until a cure has been found. It is a good idea to start collecting information on your own accord. The names of the medications are difficult to pronounce, but there are treatment hot lines that will explain the medications to you. There is also a World Wide Web site that offers detailed information about treatment and medication. You can find out more about the hot lines and Web site in the help list at the end of this book.

Medical researchers have launched a series of studies to determine the best time to start treatment of HIV. Some researchers think treatment should begin immediately after the infection has been contracted. Others believe treatment should start much later, when it is clear that the HIV has progressed to the point where it is damaging the immune system.

Until more research has been done, doctors are going to have radically different ideas about the timing of your treatment. You may be told to start treatment as soon as you are diagnosed HIV-positive, but, then again, you may be told to wait until you become HIV-symptomatic. You should ask your doctor to explain his or her views on the timing of treatment. If you are not satisfied, you should consult a second doctor.

Blood Counts

Generally, the first thing that happens when you see a doctor for HIV treatment is a count of the CD4 cells in your blood is taken. The CD4 cells are the special T cells that help your immune system fight off infection. HIV attacks the CD4 cells, leaving the body without part of its defense system. The CD4 cell count of a healthy person is about 1,000 per milliliter of blood. People with AIDS usually have a CD4 count under 200 because their immune system has been so severely weakened. Your doctor monitors your CD4 count to track the progress of the virus. If the count stays above 600, you will probably need to have your blood tested every six months. If it drops below 500, you may need blood tests more often. Treatment to slow the virus used to start when the CD4 count dropped below 500, but your doctor might recommend starting treatment earlier when your immune system is still strong. Ask your doctor:

1. the strength of your immune system now,
2. how often your CD4 count should be taken,
3. what count your CD4 should be before you start taking medication,
4. whether you should be given certain tests to monitor your progress.

The RNA PCR Test

One of the new tools in HIV treatment is the RNA PCR test recently approved for general use by the Food and Drug Administration. It is sometimes referred to as the viral load test because it takes a direct measurement of the strength of HIV in your system. The test targets RNA, the part of the HIV that knows how to make more virus and programs its growth. Doctors are using the PCR test to check the health of people with HIV and to see if anti-HIV medication is working against the virus. The results of the PCR test are given as the number of HIV RNA copies per milliliter of blood. Levels of tolerable HIV RNA are still under discussion. A group of doctors called the International AIDS Society USA have proposed that keeping the viral load below 5,000 may be a good goal for HIV treatment. One study has shown that the PCR test is a more accurate marker of the progression of the disease than CD4 cell counts.

Combination Therapy

Medication for HIV always includes the use of drugs that inhibit the growth of the virus. Because HIV is a retro-virus, these drugs are sometimes spoken of as antiretro-virals. When the first antiretrovirals were developed, the patient was given the one most likely to help him or her. This was usually AZT, known by its generic name as zidovudine, or by its brand name, Retrovir. As more drugs were discovered, researchers began to combine them to try to develop a more powerful medication against HIV. Their experiments showed that a combination of two or three anti-HIV drugs is more successful in stopping HIV than any drug taken alone. What is called combination therapy is now the standard of care for people with HIV.

All the drugs used in combination therapy are antiretrovirals, but they do not have the same chemical structure. Some are nucleoside analogs; others are protease inhibitors, and one is a non-nucleoside reverse transcriptase inhibitor (NNRTI). The approved nucleoside analogs are AZT (Retrovir), ddI (Videx), ddC (HIVID), d4T (Zerit), and 3TC (Epivir). The approved protease inhibitors are indinavir (Crixivan), nelfinavir (Viracept), saquinavir (Invirase), and ritonavir (Norvir). The approved non-nucleoside reverse transcriptase inhibitor is nevirapine (Viramune).

The differences in the chemical structure of the drugs are all important to combination therapy. It does not combine brands of medication; it combines drugs that have differing abilities to fight HIV. Each of the three types of drug stops the virus at a different stage of its growth. This means that the drugs have a massive impact on the disease when they are taken in combination with one another. Though treatment sometimes involves only two drugs, a combination of three drugs in which one is a protease inhibitor is considered to be the most effective means of treating HIV. It has prolonged the lives of patients at an advanced stage of the disease, and even helped them recover strength and vitality.

You should ask your doctor about the danger of long-term use of HIV drugs before you begin combination therapy. The drugs can produce side effects so disturbing, some patients are forced to abandon the treatment. Nevirapine (Viramune) can cause a rash. AZT can cause loss of muscle, dizziness, tongue sores, and loss of speech, among other problems. None of the drugs is free of side effects, and since they are new, no one can predict the long-term effects to patients. During combination therapy, you will need lab tests to check your body's response to the drugs.

No matter what combination of medications you are on, you will have to find a way to remind yourself when to take them and how much to take. The following methods are two of the more common. Each person must find the method that works best for him or her.

- Make a chart listing the medications for the day. Then, when the medication is ingested, check it off on the chart.
- Place the day's dosages in one spot every morning, then take the medicine until it is all gone.

You may want to use an alarm clock to remind you when to take your medication. Some people find that beepers are also useful for this purpose.

Whichever way you choose, *be consistent!* Never stop taking a medication unless your doctor says it is okay. Taking drugs for HIV is not like taking aspirin or vitamins where it is okay to skip a day. Because you cannot kill HIV (but only slow down or stop its growth), skipping one day could mean the growth of many HIV cells, no matter how great you are feeling. The new HIV cells may turn out to be resistant to the drugs and your progress may come to an abrupt halt. If your progress is interrupted, you may find it difficult to restart.

Combination therapy is a new method of treatment for HIV that can work wonders but has several problems. It can cause dangerous side effects. It doesn't work for everyone. In one study 15 percent of the patients failed to respond to combination therapy. Those who are helped live in constant fear that the virus will become resistant to the drugs. You should ask your doctor:

1. which combination of drugs has the best chance of reducing the amount of HIV in your body for the longest time;
2. the options available to you if the combination stops working;
3. the possible side effects of the medications;
4. available tests to monitor your body's response to the drugs;
5. how often you should take the medication, and for how long;
7. the health consequences should you forget to take your medication;
8. the cost of the medication.

Combination therapy is expensive. A year of it may cost $12,000 or more. If you are not covered by private or government health insurance, you have two options:

- Try to get medication through a drug company that has a compassionate-use or expanded-access program for seriously ill people who cannot afford regular treatment.
- Volunteer for a clinical trial for HIV-positive children and adolescents. Be aware that this involves risks. The trials are conducted to determine the effects and safety of experimental medication. If you volunteer for a trial, you will have to follow the treatment program set by the researchers and live with much uncertainty.

The drugs provided through compassionate-use and expanded-access programs are also experimental. For more information ask your doctor or call a treatment hot line.

Strengthening the Immune System

Antabuse is a drug used to treat alcoholism. It has also been used to stabilize CD4 cell counts. Its side effects include an allergic reaction to products containing alcohol (including mouthwash), stomach cramps if taken on an empty stomach, and a slightly metallic taste in the mouth.

Trexan is used to stimulate the production of endorphins. Its side effects include possible liver problems.

Tagamet appears to increase the production of CD4 cells. It is commonly taken for ulcers. Its side effects include diarrhea, nausea, and vomiting. It also limits the absorption of hydrochloric acid, which can cause stomach pain.

Neupogen is an anti-cancer drug, now being used on an experimental basis for HIV treatment. It stimulates the production of new white blood cells. It is expensive and can cause nausea, bone pain, and rash.

Not all doctors will offer you the full range of options. You may need to ask for an option that you have heard about, as well as for any new drugs or treatments available.

Infections or Diseases That May Affect You

You should have already had your childhood immunizations such as DPT (against diphtheria, whooping cough, and tetanus), IPV (against polio), and MMR (against mumps, measles, and rubella). If you have not had all of these immunizations, tell your doctor.

- Chicken pox is a common childhood illness. Chicken pox comes from the same virus as shingles: herpes zoster. If you have not had chicken pox and are HIV-positive, you need to avoid people who have been exposed to chicken pox. To avoid in this case means not to be in the same room unless you have no other choice. Someone who has been exposed to chicken pox can pass the virus on during the tenth to the twenty-first day after exposure. To be on the safe side, you should avoid anyone with the virus until all of the chicken pox have crusted over. If a sibling or someone else in your household has chicken pox, keep them out of your room. Do not use towels used by someone infected with chicken pox. If you are HIV-positive and have been exposed to chicken pox, call your doctor immediately. Medication can reduce serious complications from chicken pox if it is given soon enough after exposure.

• Tuberculosis is not uncommon in people who are HIV-positive. You can catch tuberculosis (TB) by being around someone who has it. It is spread by airborne germs. If you are HIV-positive, the weakness of your immune system may make it easier for you to contract TB than for someone who is not HIV-positive. TB may be active or dormant (inactive). The usual test for TB is a skin test (PPD), but for people who are HIV-positive that test is not always reliable. If your doctor suspects you have been exposed to TB but the skin test is negative, you may be asked to have a chest X ray.

The treatment for dormant TB is isoniazid (INH) every day for an entire year. No matter how you feel, you must take isoniazid for the full time. The side effects can include nausea, vomiting, and liver damage. A form of vitamin B$_6$, pyridoxine, may be prescribed to reduce the side effects.

If you have active TB, you will probably be asked to take INH and the drug rifampin (Rifadin). Rifampin can cause your tears, urine, and sweat to be orange in color. Rifampin may cause other drugs to go through the body faster than normal, requiring an increase in the dosages of those drugs. There are certain HIV medicines that someone who has HIV and TB cannot take because of drug reactions. To lessen your chances of contracting TB, avoid closed, poorly ventilated rooms.

Ask your doctor:

1. about the benefits and side effects of any medication,
2. about the costs of treatment and medication,
3. how often you should have a TB test,
4. how to limit your chances of getting TB,
5. whether your family should be tested for TB.

- Toxoplasmosis is caused by a parasite that lives in raw or undercooked red meat and cat waste. Many people in the United States carry the parasite in their bodies, but it remains inactive unless the immune system is weakened. The test for toxoplasmosis is called titration. Your doctor may order a baseline toxoplasmosis titer to determine whether or not the parasite is in your system.

The treatment is usually a combination of the drugs pyrimethamine, clindamycin, and sulfadiazine. The side effects of these drugs are nausea, vomiting, fever, and weakness. If you experience any of these side effects, call your doctor. If you are HIV-positive, eat only meat that is thoroughly cooked and stay away from cat litter boxes.

Ask your doctor:

1. about a baseline toxoplasmosis titer,
2. about the benefits of any medication,
3. about the costs of treatment and medication,
4. about the side effects of any medication,
5. how to care for animals and avoid infection.

• Pneumonia is another infection that frequently occurs in people who are HIV-positive. The lungs have numerous CD4 cells; when the CD4 count goes down, so does the ability to resist lung infections.

   The most common form of pneumonia among people who are HIV-positive is *Pneumocystis carinii* (PCP). Many people who contract PCP are unaware of it because it can take several weeks to develop. The symptoms are shortness of breath, a dry cough, and perhaps a fever. Always consult your doctor if you have a cough. To test for PCP, your doctor will probably order a chest X ray. You may also be given a breathing test to see if your lungs are inflamed.

   The usual treatment for PCP is TMP-SMX (trimethoprim-sulfamethoxazole). Its brand names are Bactrim and Septra. The side effects include a rash, nausea, and liver damage. If diagnosed in the early stages, PCP almost always can be cured. PCP is not contagious.

Ask your doctor:

1. about the benefits of medication,
2. about the costs of treatment and medications,
3. about the side effects of medication,
4. how to recognize PCP.

• Syphilis is an STD that is not uncommon in people who have contracted HIV from sexual intercourse. Syphilis can be treated with penicillin. If you have syphilis, you should notify anyone you may have exposed to the disease through unprotected intercourse or shared needles or syringes. Talk to your doctor if you think you may have been in contact with someone who has a venereal disease.

Ask your doctor:

1. about the benefits of medications,
2. about the costs of treatment and medications,
3. about the side effects of medications,
4. about testing and treatment options for STDs,
5. about the symptoms of STDs,
6. how to avoid contracting or spreading a venereal disease,
7. who will be told if you do have an STD.

• Hepatitis B is a liver inflammation caused by a DNA virus. It is contracted the same way as HIV, by the exchange of body fluids through sexual contact or exchange of blood. There is no cure for hepatitis B, and it can cause severe liver damage. A vaccine is available against hepatitis B, although it is expensive.

Ask your doctor:

1. about testing for hepatitis,
2. about the benefits of medications,
3. about the cost of treatment and medications,
4. about the hepatitis vaccine,
5. about the side effects of medications,
6. who in your household should get the hepatitis vaccine.

- Influenza. If you are HIV-positive, you are more susceptible to lung infections. Stay away from people with the flu. Also ask your doctor about getting a flu shot. Because flu symptoms can be confused with those of PCP, your health-care provider may recommend a flu shot every year.
- Kaposi's sarcoma (KS) is a tumor on a blood vessel. The symptoms are purplish or blackish nodules on the skin. Some people consider KS a sure sign of HIV. About 8 percent of the people newly diagnosed with AIDS develop KS as their initial reaction.

  Long before KS became associated with people with AIDS, it was known as a disease of elderly men, especially those of Italian or European Jewish heritage. The KS tumors usually appeared on the legs and were not particularly serious. KS acts differently on people who are HIV-positive. It can show up on the skin, where it is still relatively harmless, and on internal organs. It is most frequently found in people who contracted HIV from unprotected anal intercourse. The good news is that the percentage of HIV-positive people who develop KS is declining every year.

This may seem to be a lot of information to absorb. Being a teenager does not mean that you have no interest or responsibility in your treatment. Sometimes doctors talk to your parents as if you were not in the room. You need to know what is going on. You are the one who is being treated. The more you know about your illness, the more control you have over your own life.

Treating Noninfectious Problems

Noninfectious problems are not life-threatening in themselves, but if left unattended they can cause great harm. Some of the more common noninfectious problems of someone who is HIV-positive are depression, insomnia, anxiety, nausea, and loss of appetite. All of these are treatable with medication. Depression, insomnia, and anxiety can also be treated with exercise and relaxation therapies. You must be particularly careful about nausea and loss of appetite because you do not want to lose too much weight or lose it too quickly when you are HIV-positive. If you have any of these symptoms, tell your doctor.

If you have a friend who is experiencing depression or anxiety, you can help by just being there. Ask whether your friend wants to talk. Don't criticize or challenge your friend's feelings. Don't say you understand exactly how your friend feels. You don't, unless you are also HIV-positive. Don't talk about a similar situation you were in. You weren't, unless you too are HIV-positive. Allow your friend to express his or her feelings. Listen, accept, and then give your friend a hug. Let your friend know that you are there, no matter what.

If your friend is suffering from nausea or loss of appetite, there are a few things you can do. Sometimes when people are sick, just the smell of food cooking can be unpleasant. You could cook something at home and take it to your friend's house. Make the food look appetizing. Put only small amounts on a plate. Put a flower on the table. This may sound simplistic, but studies have shown that people eat more if the atmosphere is pleasing and the food is attractively arranged. If your friend appears to be losing weight, encourage him or her to eat and drink high-protein and high-calorie foods. Offer some pudding or a milkshake. Don't nag! If your friend refuses to eat, you cannot force the issue. You can, however, remind your friend that he or she needs to stay as healthy as possible and that one of the best ways to do that is to eat a nutritious diet.

Being a friend of someone who is HIV-positive can seem like a lot of work—and it may *be* a lot of work. If you feel that it is becoming a burden, here are some things you can do to avoid feeling resentful.

1. Don't offer to do something that you don't want to do. You have an obligation to treat your friend with love, dignity, and respect, but not to stress yourself. Offering to do things you don't want to do will make you resent your friend, even though you made the suggestion.
2. Don't agree to do something you don't want to do. You have a right to say no to your friend's requests. Just say, "I'm sorry. I can't do that now," or "I really don't want to do that." If your friend continues to ask you to do such things, you might want

to rethink the basis of your friendship. Having a friend who is HIV-positive is not always simple. If you are always turning your friend down, maybe you really don't want such a close relationship. If that's true, tell your friend that you can't handle any more than you are doing already. That may hurt your friend's feelings, but it's probably better to be honest than to let resentment build up.

3. Don't promise to do something you have no intention of doing. Sometimes we find it easier at the moment to say yes than no. That isn't fair. Your friend may have been offered an opportunity to do something else but declined because of plans made with you. Agreeing to do something you don't mean to do not only frustrates your friend but also increases your resentment.

4. Don't let your friend depress you. There are bound to be sad times when a friend is HIV-positive, but there should also be happy times. If all your time with your friend is a downer, you need to say something. It may be that your friend is in a deep depression and needs professional counseling. Although you can help by listening, you are not a professional counselor. You may have to limit the time you spend with your friend if the visits always leave you depressed. Instead of visiting in person, you might call on the phone and keep the conversation short. Stress is no better for you than it is for your friend.

5. Perhaps the best way you can avoid resentment is to be honest with your friend. Although you do not know what it feels like to be HIV-positive, you do know what it feels like to be close to someone who

is. You are as much entitled to your emotions as your friend is. Being friends with someone who is sick is not always easy. You may avoid talking about certain things for fear of upsetting your friend. You may be afraid for your friend's health or future. Your friend may not understand how you feel if you don't share your feelings. Friendship is about sharing and caring. Don't let HIV come between you and your friend. Talk about it!

CHAPTER 11

Avoiding HIV

T he teenage years are times of risk and experimentation. They are times of new body sensations, new
opportunities, and increased freedom. Teenagers
think that nothing bad can happen to them. HIV and
AIDS are things other people get. But teenagers are not
adults and often do not think of the consequences of their
actions. Peer pressure plays a large role in their behavior.

Cassie's Story

Fifteen-year-old Cassie was very excited when Will
invited her to go to a party with him. Will was nineteen, and Cassie thought he was the best-looking guy
she had ever seen. At the party, Cassie saw that
almost everyone was older than she was, but they all
seemed friendly. Someone handed her a beer. Although she had never drunk beer before, everyone
else was drinking, so Cassie did too. It seemed that
every time she finished one beer, someone handed
her another.

Cassie thought it was the best evening of her life. Everyone was laughing and having a good time. Will had his arm over her shoulders and kept pulling her close. She felt very comfortable. She and Will began kissing. Somehow they ended up in a bedroom, and Will was taking off her clothes. Cassie asked him to stop, but the beer had made her so dizzy that she didn't fight back.

Cassie and her former boyfriend had been sexually active, but they had always used a condom. She asked Will about using a condom. He kissed her and said, "Oh, Cassie, honey. I really want to be with you, right next to you, not in a condom." That sounded very romantic, and Cassie forgot about all she had learned from her parents about how to say no. She and Will had unprotected sex.

Cassie was lucky. She did not contract HIV. She did, however, contract herpes simplex 2, an incurable STD. She could have just as easily have been infected with HIV.

It wasn't just one thing that made Cassie vulnerable to contracting HIV. First of all, she went to a party unsupervised by adults. Second, she drank too much. Third, she allowed Will to pressure her into having unprotected sex.

Some people might blame Cassie for all that happened. But she was a teenager, and she liked Will. It made her feel good to know that someone so good-looking wanted to spend time with her. Cassie didn't want to seem out of place, so she drank beer. The teen years are a time of experimentation; teens try out many different things during this time. Unfortunately, alcohol clouds a person's judgement and lowers inhibition. She couldn't remember how she got into the bedroom. Using alcohol or drugs in a situation like this increases the chances that sex will occur. It decreases your inhibitions and can make you take chances you know you shouldn't.

Cassie also allowed herself to be pressured into having sex without a condom, something she had never done before. Peer pressure is a fact of life for many teenagers. Unfortunately, it can also be deadly.

More and more teenagers are delaying sex until they are in a long-term monogamous relationship. Before you have sex with anyone, you should know that person well enough to talk about the danger of pregnancy, sexually transmitted diseases, and the future. Teenagers make up the group with the fastest-growing incidence of HIV. If you are uncomfortable talking with your partner about being safe, you need to rethink having sex with him or her.

Two basic rules can help you avoid HIV: Don't have sex right now, and don't do drugs.

If you have trouble following those rules, then at least take the following safety measures:

1. Avoid any kind of unprotected sex, male to female, male to male, female to female; HIV is spread through anal, oral, and vaginal intercourse. Always use a latex condom when having sex. Any lubricants must be water-based; all oil-based lubricants breakdown latex. The condom reduces the risk of contracting HIV or any other sexually transmitted disease, and also the risk of pregnancy. If someone wants you to have sex without a condom, say no. An STD or pregnancy lasts a lot longer than it takes to put on a condom. If you are old enough

to have sex, you are old enough to think about the consequences of unprotected sex and to do something about them.

2. Be aware of common cuts and sores in the mouth, hands, vagina, and anus of your own body and the body of your sex partner. They are indications that you should not engage in sexual activity. If you do, take extra precautions such as wearing latex gloves. The virus can be transmitted through cuts and sores.

3. Avoid casual sex. The more people you have sex with, the greater your chances of contracting HIV. When you have sex with someone, you are also having sex with everyone they have ever had sex with and everyone their partners have ever had sex with.

4. Avoid having sex with people you do not know or people who you know use intravenous drugs, have any sexually transmitted disease, or have casual sex.

5. Avoid situations where you may be pressured to engage in risky behavior. If you go to a place where there will be drugs or alcohol or that is unsupervised by adults, think carefully about what you do.

You can take control of your life by making the right decisions. If someone pressures you to use drugs or have sex, you can say no in a variety of ways. If the person continues pressuring you, you need to think about that relationship. Are his or her wants and needs more important than your own sense of well-being?

Although the common way to contract HIV is through unprotected sex or shared needles, there has recently been some concern about teenagers contracting HIV as a result of body-piercing. Body-piercing is usually unregulated, which means that no safeguards are in place for health standards and safety precautions. If you are thinking about having your body pierced or having a tattoo, be extra careful about where you go. All professional piercers and tattoo artists should use one-time sterilized needles for each client. A needle that has been used on someone infected with HIV and has not been cleaned is a sure way to contract the virus. Sharing blood like "blood brothers" is also a way to get HIV if one of you is infected.

HIV can happen to anyone—gay or straight, old or young. People do not set out to become infected. Getting HIV is the result of a mistake. Everyone makes mistakes. The problem is that with HIV one mistake is all it takes.

CHAPTER ◇ 12

New Developments

n 1981 AIDS was a mysterious new disease. There was
no medication for AIDS. There was not even a way to
test for it. Doctors knew you had AIDS when your
immune system broke down and minor problems like a
cold became major problems like pneumonia. It was most
common among homosexual men.

Now, sixteen years later, almost everything about AIDS
has changed. It is a problem for the entire population,
straight and gay, and it is a problem that is on its way to being
solved. The HIV antibody test was approved by the Food
and Drug Administration in 1985, and two years later, AZT,
the first effective AIDS medication, was also approved by
the Food and Drug Administration.

In 1995 progress began to shoot forward at a rate that
left people both stunned and relieved. New tests, new
drugs, and new ways to use the drugs were unveiled. Their
success has been dramatic. Some experts claim AIDS
should now be regarded as a chronic illness that is not life-
threatening if it is properly treated. Others are more cautious, but many agree that the future of people with HIV
looks brighter than ever before.

The Home Tests for HIV

The Food and Drug Administration approved the sale of kits for home HIV testing in 1996, after a lengthy review process. You can find these kits in your local pharmacy or clinic. Direct mail order from the manufacturer is also an option.

It is clear that the Food and Drug Administration's approval of home tests marks a turning point in the history of HIV. Hopefully, the greater convenience, privacy, and speed offered by home tests will result in people, especially teenagers, feeling more comfortable about getting tested, which in turn will result in more people getting treatment before they are HIV-symptomatic.

There is another way besides blood tests to determine if you are HIV-positive. A test using fluids from inside the mouth, with the brand name Orasure, has been recently approved.

The PCR Test

PCR tests are playing a crucial role in the treatment of HIV patients and in medical research into the disease. One type of PCR test is also referred to as the viral load test.

The PCR test that is currently being used is distributed under the name Amplicor HIV-1 Monitor test. Another, the Chiron DNA test, has shown promising results in clinical trials and has been approved for routine use.

The PCR test is a direct outgrowth of research into the genetic structure of HIV. It monitors the amount of HIV RNA in the infected person's bloodstream. RNA is the part of HIV that knows how to reproduce the virus.

Scientists have never before had a direct gauge of

the strength of the disease. The PCR test has already led to discoveries of great importance to HIV-positive adolescents, as well as anyone else recently diagnosed with HIV.

Because it generally takes years for an HIV-positive person to become symptomatic, scientists have operated under the assumption that HIV multiplies slowly. The PCR test has shown that this is not the case. As soon as HIV enters the system, it "spikes," sending out billions of cells. The "spike" doesn't affect the person's health because his or her immune system is still intact. It fights off the HIV and only very gradually loses the battle against the invader.

The discovery of the HIV "spike" has intensified controversy over the timing of drug treatment. Some experts now believe that treatment should begin as soon as possible after diagnosis in order to help the immune system knock the virus out of the body. Thus far, this approach is showing promising results and is providing hope for everyone in effectively fighting HIV and delaying the onset of AIDS.

The New Anti-HIV Medication

There is no single wonder drug in HIV treatment, but the protease inhibitor is, far and away, the most powerful of the drugs now available for general use. They work by blocking a part of HIV called protease. When protease is blocked, HIV makes benign copies of itself that can't infect new cells. The first protease inhibitor was introduced in 1995 under the brand name Invirase. It is also called saquinavir. Since 1995, the Food and Drug Administration has approved three more protease inhibitors:

indinavir (Crixivan), nelfinavir (Viracept), and ritonavir (Norvir).

Used on its own, a protease inhibitor would be an effective drug against HIV. Dr. David Ho and his team of scientists pioneered much of this research. Dr. Ho's discovery was that it can be combined with other anti-HIV drugs such as AZT to form powerful "cocktails." A clinical trial Dr. Ho supervised at the Diamond Institute showed that patients began to improve after taking the three-drug "cocktails" for a few weeks. They were not cured, but they did make remarkable comebacks.

No earlier method of treatment had accomplished anything comparable to the near cure of the three-drug mixtures. Before David Ho's discovery, the most you could expect from medication was a slowing of the disease's progress. Now there was medication that could reverse its spread through the body. The viral load of some patients became so low, it could not be detected through PCR testing. However, this does not mean that the person is cured.

Combination therapy with protease inhibitors was first introduced in 1996. Within a few months, combination therapy had helped thousands of people and had become the standard treatment for AIDS. Because of the success of the new therapy, many experts claim that AIDS will soon be approached as a "chronic management illness" like diabetes.

They hope that AIDS will soon only require medication and good health care and will be fatal in less cases. We will not know if this is really true until doctors and patients have had many more years of experience with combination therapy.

The Next Step in Combination Therapy

After Dr. Ho completed his first study of 3-drug combination therapy, he started another in which he studied its impact on the "spike" of early HIV infection. The results were successful.

The "cocktails" did lower the viral load of the patients, but several questions emerged. The PCR test monitors the amount of HIV in the blood stream. Most HIV is found in other parts of the body, especially in the lymph system. Even if only a few HIV cells survive drug treatment, they have the power to multiply and endanger the person once again.

This complicates the issue of early treatment. If there is no certainty that the HIV has been totally destroyed, when do you stop the drugs? And if you stop the drugs, will they be effective against a fresh attack of HIV?

These questions are at the center of current research into HIV. There is great concern about HIV's ability to develop a resistance to the drugs. If any of the drugs are stopped, it is usually not effective when it is tried a second time. Scientists are trying to increase the number and variety of anti-HIV drugs so they have weapons against resistant strains of the virus. For example, some scientists are trying to develop a new type of drug that would target the genetic structure of HIV. Molecules called chemokines are the focus of another group of scientists. Meanwhile, there is fear that once combination therapy is started, it cannot be stopped, even if the person's immune system is healthy.

*   *   *

No one knows what the long range effects of combination therapy will be. All of the drugs have side effects ranging from diarrhea to rashes to anemia that pose health problems. If the person requires medication for other conditions, there is likely to be difficulty in finding one that interacts well with the anti-HIV drugs.

A Vaccine Against HIV

Many scientists regard the development of an inexpensive vaccine as the number one priority of HIV research. They cite the example of the Salk vaccine that removed the threat of polio. And they point to two facts that tend to be overlooked in the excitement over the recent breakthroughs in research.

1. The new drug therapy is very expensive. It usually costs $12,000 to $15,000 each year and in some cases the total may be even higher.

2. HIV has become a global epidemic. It is found all over the world in places including Africa, Asia, the Caribbean, Europe, Latin America, the Middle East, and North America. At the end of 1996, the United Nations estimated that more than 22 million people had contracted HIV. Most get the virus through heterosexual contact. Many are women and children living in poverty.

Cost restricts the use of the new drugs to a small fraction of the people with HIV. The disease continues to menace the lives of those unable to get up-to-date medication. A vaccine would not solve this problem, but it would halt the further spread of the disease.

So the future is not as bleak as it once was for people who are HIV-positive. Every day researchers learn more about the virus. If you are HIV-positive, take care of yourself and think positively. There is a future for you. If you are friends with someone who is HIV-positive, remind your friend that there is hope. Good luck and remember that you are not alone.

Glossary

AIDS (acquired immune deficiency syndrome) A stage of HIV disease when the immune system has been damaged by the virus and is unable to fight infection. Physical symptoms of diseases associated with the HIV virus, such as PCP and thrush, must also be evident on the body.

antibodies Proteins in the blood which recognize and block foreign substances and infections.

antiretroviral A substance that stops or suppresses the activity of a retrovirus such as HIV.

asymptomatic Infection without symptoms. The infection is present in the body, antibodies are formed against the infection, however no signs or symptoms are outwardly apparent.

autoimmune disease A disease which arises from and is directed against an individual's own body and organs.

AZT (zidovudine, Retrovir) The first and one of the most common drugs used to treat HIV. It is now most often used in combination with other anti-HIV drugs. It is approved for preventing transmission of HIV from mother to child.

combination therapy The use of two or more drugs at the same time as treatment.

condom A flexible protective sheath placed over the penis before intercourse. When used properly, those made of latex can prevent pregnancy and the spread of disease.

expanded access Programs designed to make experimental drugs available on a wide basis to people who do not qualify for the drug trials or who live too far from a trial site.

hairy leukoplakia   A whitish, slightly raised lesion that appears on the side of the cheeks, gums, or tongue.

helper cells (T4 cells)   A subset of T cells that are vital for antibody production and starting many other immune responses. The number of T4 cells measures the health of an HIV-positive person's immune system.

HIV disease   A term used to describe a variety of symptoms and signs found in people who are HIV-positive. These may include fever, weight loss, swollen lymph nodes, and or fungus infections of the throat and mouth.

inhibitor   A drug, chemical, or substance, that blocks something from happening.

nevirapine (Viramune)   The only approved anti-HIV, non-nucleoside reverse transcriptase inhibitor (NNRTI). HIV develops resistance to this drug quickly so it is approved for use in combination with other HIV drugs.

night sweats   Extreme sweating during sleep.

nucleoside analog   A class of drugs used to treat HIV which creates an artificial copy of a nucleoside. The virus mistakes this for a real nucleoside and uses it to build new viral DNA. The analog prevents continued production of the virus. Common types include AZT, ddI, and ddC.

opportunistic infection   An infection that takes advantage of a weakened immune system.

PCR (polymerase chain reaction assay)   An approved viral load test that measures the amount of HIV in a blood sample. The result provides information about the risk of disease progression, and determines how well an anti-HIV treatment is working.

protease inhibitor   A class of drugs which stop protease, an enzyme needed by the HIV virus for replication, from working. Used in combination therapy to stop the HIV virus from growing. Studies have shown that it can greatly reduce the amount of HIV in the blood, particularly when combined with other anti-HIV drugs. Common types include indinavir, nelfinavir, saquinavir, and ritonavir.

resistance The ability of a disease to overcome a drug. The disease develops strains of the virus that are no longer debilitated by the drug.

semen Sperm-carrying fluid released through the penis at the climax of sexual activity.

side effects The action or effect of a drug other than that which is desired. The term usually refers to negative or undesirable effects, such as headache, nausea, or rash.

T cell White blood cells that play an important part in the immune system. Because HIV kills T cells, the number of these cells is consistently measured in people who are HIV-positive.

transfusion The process of giving blood, or parts of the blood, from one person to another.

vaccine Medicine given to a person by a doctor to increase immunity and to prevent a particular disease.

virus Small living organism that can grow and increase in the body and cause infection.

white blood cells Part of the immune system that protects the body against foreign substances, such as disease-producing microorganisms.

Where to Go for Help

AIDS and Adolescent Network of New York
666 Broadway, Suite 520
New York, NY 10012
(212) 505-9115

AIDS Treatment Data Network World Wide Web:
http://www.aidsnyc.org/network

National Black Leadership Commission on AIDS
105 East 22nd Street, Suite 711
New York, NY 10010
(212) 614-0023

Hetrick Martin Institute for Gay and Lesbian Youth
2 Astor Place
New York, NY 10003
(212) 674-2400

Hispanic AIDS Forum
184 Fifth Avenue, 7th Floor
New York, NY 10010
(212) 741-9797

National Hemophilia Foundation
110 Greene St., Ste. 303
New York, NY 10012
(212) 219-8180

CANADA

AIDS Committee Toronto (ACT)
399 Church Street
(416) 340-2437

AIDS Vancouver
1272 Richard Street
Vancouver, British Columbia V6B 3G2
(604) 687-2437

AIDS Network of Edmonton Society
#201 11456 Jasper Avenue
Edmonton, Alberta T5K 0MI
(403) 488-5742

Metro Area Committee on AIDS (MACAIDS)
5675 Spring Garden Road
Suite 305
Halifax, Nova Scotia B3J 1H1
(902) 425-4882

Hassle Free Clinics/AIDS Committee
556 Church Street #2
Toronto, Ontario M4Y 2E3
(416) 922-0603

SUPPORT HOT LINES

AIDS for Teens: (800) 234-8336
Hyacinth (Spanish): (800) 433-0254
National HIV and AIDS: (800) 342-2437
National AIDS (Spanish): (800) 344-742
National AIDS TTY/TTD Service: (800) 243-7889

TREATMENT HOT LINES

Experimental AIDS Therapies: (800) 874-2572
Project Inform: (800) 822-7422

FOR MORE INFORMATION ON HIV OR AIDS, CONTACT:

Centers for Disease Control and Prevention (CDC)
1600 Clifton Rd. NE
Atlanta, GA 30333
404-639-3311
404-332-4555 (Voice Information System)

For Further Reading

Anonymous Teenager. *It Happened to Nancy*. Beatrice Sparks, ed. New York: Avon Books, 1994.

Arrick, Fran. *What You Don't Know Can Kill You*. New York: Bantam, 1992.

Blake, Jeanne. *Risky Times: How to Be AIDS Free and Stay Healthy: A Guide for Teenagers*. New York: Workman Pub., 1990.

Davis, Christopher. *Philadelphia: A Novel*. New York: Bantam Books, 1993.

Ford, Michael Thomas. *101 Questions and Answers About AIDS: A Guide for Young People*. New York: Young Discovery Books, 1992.

Harris, E. Lynn. *Just as I Am: A Novel*. New York: Doubleday, 1994.

Johnson, Earvin "Magic." *What You Can Do to Avoid AIDS*. New York: Times Books, 1992.

Johnson, Fenton. *Scissors, Paper, Rock*. New York: Bantam Books, 1993.

Kittredge, Mary. *Teens with AIDS Speak Out*. Englewood Cliffs, NJ: Julian Messner, 1991.

National Directory of Children, Youth and Family Services. *National Directory of Resources on HIV Infection/AIDS*. Longmont, CO, 1994.

Nelson, Teresa. *Earthshine: A Novel*. New York: Orchard Books, 1994.

Porte, Barbara Ann. *Something Terrible Happened: A Novel*. New York: Orchard Books, 1994.

Shilts, Randy. *And the Band Played On: Politics, People, & the AIDS Epidemic*. New York: Viking Penguin, 1993.

White, Ryan, and Marie Cunningham. *Ryan White, My Own Story.* New York: Dial Books, 1991.

Videography

"It Is What Is" Videotape with discussion guide. New York: GMHC, 1992. Available by telephone order: (212) 337-1950

Index

D

ddC (HIVID), 100
ddI (Videx), 100
dentist
requirement to notify of
HIV infection, 45, 78–79
risk of contracting HIV
from, 12–13
developments, new, 118–124
d4T (Zerit), 100
discrimination, 80–82, 83–84
doctor
family, 24
relationship with, 95–97
requirement to notify of
HIV infection, 45, 78–79
drug treatments, 1, 4–5, 7,
99–103
drug use, intravenous (IV), 14,
15, 16, 22, 63

E

education, right to, 82–83
emotions, dealing with, 31–51
exercise, 93

F

fear, 4, 29, 42–47, 62–63, 73,
75
fluconazole (Diflucan), 90
Food and Drug
Administration, 99, 120
friends
telling of HIV status to,
70–76
telling of homosexuality to,
72–76

G

gp120 proteins, 6–7
guilt, feelings of, 39–42

H

helping a friend with HIV,
109–112
hemophilia, 11
hepatitis B, 107–108
herpes simplex, 90, 114
herpes zoster, 104
HIV (human immunodeficiency
virus)
avoiding, 113–117
difference from AIDS, 6–9
myths about, 4, 10–19
symptoms of, 7–8, 21, 52–53
in teens, 1–2
ways of contracting, 2,
10–11, 23, 115–117
HIV test, 17–18, 20–30
anonymous, 24–25, 26–27
cost of, 26, 29
ELISA (Enzyme-linked
Immunosorbent Assay),
18, 25
false positive, 18, 30
friend, to accompany to, 29
home testing, 25, 27–29, 119
negative, 17–18, 30
places to take, 25–26
positive, 6, 31
preparation for, 23–25
reasons for taking, 21–23
results of, 26–27
Western Blot, 18, 25
homosexuality and HIV, 15, 16,
39–41, 66–67, 72–76
hugging, 10, 47

I

immune system, 7, 31
indinavir (Crixivan), 100, 121